A
HANDBOOK
FOR **I**NTERIOR
DESIGNERS

A
HANDBOOK
FOR INTERIOR
DESIGNERS

Jenny Gibbs

WARD LOCK

A WARD LOCK BOOK
First published in the UK 1995 by
Ward Lock
Wellington House
125 Strand
LONDON WC2R 0BB

A Cassell Imprint

Distributed in the United States by
Sterling Publishing Co., Inc.
387 Park Avenue South, New York
NY 10016–8810

A British Library Cataloguing in Publication Data
block for this book may be obtained from the
British Library.

ISBN 0 7063-7638-2

Typeset by Keystroke, Jacaranda Lodge,
Wolverhampton
Printed and bound in Great Britain by
The Bath Press

ACKNOWLEDGEMENTS

I would like to thank the following
colleagues from KLC: Simon Cavelle, Jill
Blake, Ruth Pretty, Mary Laurie, Debby
Thurston and Christine Brazier for their
professional advice and Natasha
Whitehouse-Jansen for her good-humoured
help with typing and retyping the
manuscript. My thanks, too, to my family for
once again being wonderfully tolerant of a
bad-tempered author.

Black and white illustrations courtesy of:
Armitage Shanks Ltd. (tel. 01543 490253)
p. 39; Laura Ashley **p. 66**; Depitch Designs
(Avon Classic brass bedstead; tel. 0181 687
0867) **p. 77**; Dulux (tel. 01753 550555)
pp. 12, 15 (from the Naturals Collection)
p. 40; Fired Earth (tel. 01295 812088) **p. 13**;
Katherine Gill **p. 81**; C.P. Hart (tel. 0171 902
1000) **p. 18**; Houses and Interiors **p. 62**; Ikea
Ltd. **p. 80**; KLC Design Studio **p. 105** (left
and right); Magnet Kitchens (Shaker; tel.
0800 555835) **p. 54**; Tara McLaren **p. 103**;
MFI (Westminster, from the Hygena range;
MFI Freepages tel. 0500 192192) **p. 53**; Pella
Doors (tel. 0171 730 6141) **p. 37**; Pamela
Sarna **p. 32**; Ward Lock **p. 3**; The Water
Monopoly (tel. 0171 624 2636) **p. 81**.

Frontispiece: *Bathrooms do not need to be
confined to small internal spaces. Here the bath
is placed in the centre of the room with a
relaxing view over the gardens. Carefully
chosen furniture and accessories contribute to
the contemplative air.*

CONTENTS

INTRODUCTION

In Victorian times the upholsterer filled the role of interior designer to a certain extent, providing not only upholstery but curtains and loose covers and, in addition, access to a whole range of skilled craftsmen. The upholsterer would oversee the entire decorative project, and this resulted in a fairly coordinated look. After the First World War, many women set themselves up as interior decorators on a fee-paying basis, and then helped *nouveau riche* clients who lacked the appropriate heirlooms and know-how for their new station in life.

Many of today's leading interior designers and decorators received no formal training, but learnt about the business by serving what was virtually an apprenticeship with an established design company. However, the technical advances in areas such as lighting, the vast ranges of products that are available and the increasing number of would-be designers have meant that interior design has become a profession in its own right. The trained professional will be up to date with current trends and methods, will know how to oversee all the installations on site to ensure a durable, high quality result and will be able to present their creative ideas to the client in a proficient and effective way.

Specialist home furnishing magazines, exhibitions and houses open to the public have made many home owners well informed about interior decoration, but most lack the confidence and time to plan and carry out a scheme on their own, and they therefore seek the guidance of a professional interior decorator or designer.

One popular misconception is that the work of an interior designer is chiefly

The interior designer will provide schemes to complement the architectural style of a property. A period country house will need harmonious styles and colours.

concerned with choosing matching fabrics, wallcoverings and floorings. In fact, the decorative scheme is often the last part of the presentation a designer puts together for a project. A full design project would start with taking the all-important brief from the client, followed by a careful survey and measuring up the space involved, so that the designer has the information to set about finding the right design solutions to the client's brief. The resulting scheme has then to be put together in an appropriate presentation form – perhaps plans with furniture layouts, sample boards and visuals – to communicate, and indeed sell, the designer's ideas to the client. If the scheme is accepted, the designer will probably be required to manage the project through to its completion.

Some people confuse the role of the interior designer with that of the decorator. In general, the designer is mainly concerned with the planning of the space while the decorator is responsible for the surface decoration of that space. That said, however, the two roles are often completely interchangeable. Both the designer and the decorator aim to provide their clients with an environment that really satisfies their requirements and to plan and supervise the works involved in achieving it.

Safety, of course, is vital and is the designer's responsibility. The designer would also organize the various contractors and craftsmen involved in the project and source appropriate decorative materials and accessories. Accomplishing these tasks requires not only creative flair, but also good

Research is an important part of an interior designer's work, particularly when period renovation is involved. Symmetry and proportion were vital factors in Georgian interiors.

administrative and communication skills, the ability to manage people and a considerable amount of stamina and humour. This book is not about taste or style; instead, it is intended to give sound guidelines and fundamental principles for design practice. It will also reveal some of the complexities of this type of work. Full training in interior design can take up to four years, and even then experience plays a vital part. The learning process never ceases, and it is definitely not possible to become an interior designer over night!

The usual entry route into the profession is via a degree in interior design preceded by a foundation course. However, mature students with valuable experience or degrees in subjects such as marketing or business studies find these combine well with an intensive one-year training course in interior design and decoration to provide an entrée into the profession.

There is no set career route within the profession, but the opportunities increase from contributing to a small part of a project to running your own. It can require very hard work and long hours, and starting salaries are not overly high, but at the end of the day it is an exciting, satisfying and rewarding profession.

CHAPTER ONE

TAKING THE BRIEF

Taking the brief is an absolutely vital stage in any project. If you do not get a really thorough brief from the client in the first place, it is unlikely that you will be able to carry out the project successfully. It is important to set up a good working relationship with your client from the start and to get a clear understanding of what is required and the constraints, financial or otherwise, that might affect the project.

There are two types of client: the private client, who wants his or her domestic interiors to be redecorated or refurbished, which is quite personal work, and the commercial client, whose requirements will be more impersonal but will offer greater scope for the planning of space. Some clients will give a clear, easy-to-follow brief, but in most cases you will need to ask careful questions and to be extremely observant so that you extract the necessary information. In short, you need to be a consultant and psychologist rolled into one. Remember, however, that you should never impose your own ideas on your client – you are there to advise and to interpret the client's ideas.

THE INITIAL ENQUIRY

From the first point of contact with your client, your professionalism should be to the fore. Carefully record the main points of the first conversation, which may be a telephone conversation. Try to establish whether you are going to be given a proper brief or whether it is merely a consultation. Follow up this conversation with a confirming letter, clarifying the situation to avoid any misunderstandings later. If it is just a consultation, include in your letter a note of your fee for the service. If both the husband and wife are to be clients try to get them both to attend the briefing. It is also helpful to establish who will be the decision-maker and who will be paying the bills. This again will help avoid confusion or misunderstanding later on.

Methods of charging are discussed in Chapter 11. How you charge will largely depend on what the job entails. In some instances it may just be a consultancy fee, which would be either a flat fee or charged on an hourly basis. For instance, you may be asked to advise a couple who have just moved into a flat that has been redecorated in a very bland way for the rental market. The curtains, carpets and fittings may be of reasonably good quality and your clients may not have the budget to start afresh. Carefully chosen paint colours, adjustments to the way the curtains are hung, new tie-backs, borders for definition, one or two throws over the upholstery and a few well-placed accessories will make an enormous difference, and this work can be done for a modest flat consultancy fee.

On other occasions, if you are supplying a lot of soft furnishings, for example, your fee would come from the mark-up. On large projects it is often appropriate to charge a small percentage on the total sum spent on the project.

THE CLIENT MEETING

Nothing makes a worse impression than arriving late and flustered, so prepare carefully for the meeting. Check travel and parking arrangements beforehand and make sure that you do not lose valuable time. Mid-morning is an ideal time for meetings because it avoids both awkward mealtimes and the possibility of you or your client having had too lengthy a lunch. Before you leave the office, make sure you have all the equipment you need and a prepared questionnaire. Start the observation process by carefully observing the exterior of the property – its age, style and position – before you go inside.

At this initial meeting your client may be concerned that you are going to suggest inordinately expensive schemes that are well beyond their budget. So often, very simple changes and additions can make all the difference. A room can be transformed with subtle use of colour, rearrangement of existing furniture, the introduction of atmospheric lighting (free-standing up-lighters are particularly effective for this purpose) or mirrors strategically placed to enlarge the space, none of which need cost the earth.

During the briefing your aim is to establish exactly what has to be done and exactly what the clients want you to provide. If they are in the process of purchasing the property, it is wise to try to establish when completion is due. Ask if they plan to move in before the work is completed, and try to get some idea of the length of time they envisage living there. Find out what their priorities are. For example, if their budget is not sufficient to do the whole house immediately, you could perhaps suggest a three-year plan, starting with the rooms they feel need attention first.

Observe the clients as carefully as the interiors themselves. Factors such as age, height and weight can be important when you are choosing items like beds or seating, but you should also note the dress, lifestyle, family, pets, surroundings and so on. You really need to get a feeling for the clients' expectations and hopes. Listen to what they want, need, like or dislike. If they are uncertain what they want, ask questions that will draw out their views. It is amazing how clients will open up and how much valuable information you can glean if you approach the briefing session in a prepared, professional and relaxed manner. Encourage them to contribute their ideas and remember that, ultimately, they are the ones who are going to be living with your designs, not you. Your designs should, therefore, reflect their personalities, and they should feel entirely comfortable in the surroundings you provide. The space must work for them and any guidance from you should be given subtly.

Before you enter a property to take the brief from a client, take careful note of any exterior features, such as the balustrade, porch with pilasters and fanlight on this early nineteenth-century house.

A typical mid-nineteenth century house in San Francisco.

EQUIPMENT

A clipboard with your prepared questionnaire attached and a pen are the essentials. You could also consider taking a camera to record specific details, although you should ask permission before you use it. A paint colour swatch can be valuable for colour matching with existing items that may have to be incorporated into a new scheme. It is always useful to have a steel measuring tape with you, even if you are not doing a full measuring up exercise at the same time as taking the brief.

If the clients have not seen any of your work before, you could take a small portfolio with some appropriate examples to show them. Their reaction to this may give you some pointers towards their preferences. Another effective prop to help clients arrive at the sort of style they want is a file of 'ideas' for different rooms taken from magazines.

It is very important to gather as much information as possible at this first meeting. It is all too easy to be distracted at the time and to forget to ask something crucial. In order to avoid this, always work with prepared check lists and refer to them as a 'prompt' sheet. Your check list will include the following points, although you should have spare paper to take additional notes.

☐ Name, address, day and evening telephone and fax number of client
☐ Address and telephone number where work is to be carried out (if different from above)
☐ Client's preferred style, colours, etc

☐ Number of residents in the household – i.e. children (ages and sex), pets, parents, staff, etc
☐ Existing possessions to be included in the new scheme
☐ Lifestyle
How rooms are to be allocated
Bathrooms – how many required; how many *en suite*?
Laundry – how is this done and by whom; where is the most convenient place?
Telephones, pcs, faxes, etc – how many and in which rooms?
TVs, CD players, etc – how many and in which rooms?
Entertaining – formal or informal; numbers?
Family eating – in dining room and/or kitchen?

Storage
Any special requirements, such as space for exercising, hobbies, etc
☐ Timing – how long has been allowed for the project? How long does the client envisage living in the house/flat etc?
☐ Budget available

As you run through these points, try to get a clear picture of the way the client and the household live and the type of people they are so that you can really create the right backdrop for them.

For a commercial project, such as an office, you should adapt the form to cover the type of company, the number of employees, the number of directors' offices, the number of workstations and so on.

Find out about your client's lifestyle. Life in a country cottage will have different considerations from that in a city apartment.

Even before you measure any of the rooms which are involved in the brief you will need to do a careful analysis of the existing space.

In order to do this it is again advisable to prepare some check lists in advance so that you can simply fill in the relevant information on site. For example, for each room you will need the following useful information:

☐ **Orientation:** i.e., north, south, east, west – and quality of light
☐ **Architectural style**
☐ **Ceiling:** condition, height, beams, mouldings, ceiling rose, cornice
☐ **Walls:** condition, panelling, decorative plasterwork, dado rails
☐ **Windows:** view, style, condition, position in room
☐ **Joinery:** condition, quality, height and positions of cupboards, shelves, boxing-in, radiator casings, etc
☐ **Doors:** position, orientation, type – i.e. polished, painted, jib, panelled – type and condition of architraves
☐ **Floor:** existing, sub-floor, covering, condition
☐ **Radiators:** position, condition, boxed-in casings, position of pipes
☐ **Fireplace:** style, condition, colour, type of grate, open or closed chimney; gas supply (in case a gas fire is required); if no fireplace, does a chimney breast indicate that one may have been blocked in?
☐ **Electrics:** condition, position and number of sockets and switches, existing light fittings

It is also advantageous at this stage to make a quick, rough sketch plan of the areas relating to the project.

When you return to your office you should be able to collate all the information from your analysis of the space and the information you have gleaned from the client so that you can start planning on a room-by-room basis. You could draw up a schedule showing what can be retained and listing what redecoration and alterations are required and noting any particular constraints or problems. At this stage you should also write a letter to the client confirming your understanding of the project, setting out your fees and giving a realistic timetable. Never allow a client to persuade you to attempt to undertake a project on an unrealistic schedule – it will only lead to problems and disappointments in the long run.

As you start the planning process, bear in mind the small details that are important to the people who will have to live with your work but that are easy to overlook. Following are some room-by-room suggestions against which you can check your ideas.

Areas where water pipes have been boxed in with false panel can be used creatively to make a feature like these display shelves placed in the recess. Painting the back of the display area a darker colour than the walls sets off the objects displayed there.

Entrance halls

Mat well; mirror; chair; storage for coats, umbrellas, walking sticks, pram or pushchair, and sports equipment if applicable; table for messages, keys and so on.

Cloakrooms and bathrooms

Storage for toiletries, medicines (in a lockable cupboard); towel rails/rings; number of basins; size of bath; shower type; jacuzzi; WC; bidet; stool; chair; side table.

Kitchens

Appliances – e.g., cooker, hob, oven (single/double, etc.), refrigerator, freezer, waste disposal, dishwasher, microwave; electrical items – e.g., blender, food-processor, kettle, toaster, coffee machine; food storage; eating area and number to be seated – e.g., breakfast bar, separate table; storage for cleaning materials; any occasional seating; ventilation – e.g., duct, fan; storage for china, glass, cutlery, cookery books, wine, saucepans, casseroles, ironing board and iron; telephone, radio, TV and so on.

A well-planned kitchen makes all the difference to the busy cook. In square or rectangular kitchens, the addition of a central island unit maximizes space. It can be used as an area for cooking, washing up and a breakfast bar. The surface is attractively tiled and forms a striking contrast to the light-coloured units. The two-level island houses a sink, ceramic hob, a breakfast area and gives generous storage for saucepans in pull-out drawers below the hob.

13

Sitting room

How many people to be seated; storage required for books or display for decorative objects, etc; wallhangings and pictures; type of leisure activities carried out in the room – e.g., watching TV, listening to music, playing cards, needlepoint, working at desk, playing piano, serving drinks; built-in storage for clutter, books, TV, stereo system and other appliances.

Dining room

Numbers to be seated; shape of table; facilities required for serving, storage or display; relationship of dining room to kitchen and wine storage; how room is used – e.g., formally, at night, for lunch.

Bedrooms

How many, size and position of beds; bedside requirements – e.g., lighting; type of bed treatments; dressing table; additional furniture – e.g., desk, day bed, armchair; clothes storage required – e.g., full- or half-length hanging, racks for bags and shoes, open shelves or drawers for shirts, sweaters, underwear, accessories, hanging for belts and ties, alternative storage for seasonal clothes; full-length mirrors; dressing area separate or within bedroom; TV, radio and telephone.

Nursery and/or children's rooms or playroom

Safety; number of cots or beds; seating; lockable medicine cabinet; storage for clothes, books, toys; facilities for washing or feeding baby; area for homework.

◄ A built-in kitchen might not be appropriate for a cottage interior, and your client might want to combine modern efficiency with a traditional look.

► For many people a completely separate dining room is unnecessary. This contemporary dining area is linked to the kitchen through an arch. A dining room could also serve a dual purpose and function as a study or playroom during the day.

◄ Researching into suitable styles and selecting special pieces of furniture is an important part of an interior designer's work.

CHAPTER TWO

THE SURVEY

The survey should cover every aspect of the space designated in the brief. If you have not previously carried out a detailed analysis of the space (see Chapter 1) you should do so when you are measuring up, paying particular attention to the orientation, the quality of light and the condition of each room.

You should also carefully record any items that the client wishes to retain. Indeed, at this stage all the existing features should be recorded, because in order to carry out the planning and design work, you will require detailed plans. You must take accurate measurements for these plans. Never be tempted to rush – you will inevitably forget something or make a mistake, which could jeopardize the entire project. Make sure you note down all the necessary measurements neatly and clearly so there can be no mistakes or confusion at the drawing up stage.

Decide whether you are going to work in metric or imperial measurements and remain consistent throughout. Do not be tempted to swap half-way through, because this will cause havoc! Metric scale is the most commonly used in interior design – your scale rule will be metric – and it is much simpler to calculate when you come to draw up the plans from your survey sketch.

EQUIPMENT

For surveying and measuring you will need the following equipment:

☐ **Clip board:** preferably one with space to attach pens and pencils so that they are always to hand
☐ **Survey sheets:** should ideally be graph paper, with your analysis of the space on the reverse, because it will help you draw reasonably straight and correctly proportioned lines

☐ **Retractable steel measuring tape:** at least 5–7 metres (16–23 ft) long
☐ **Pencils:** the kind with a rubber at the end are especially useful
☐ **Pen:** with which you feel comfortable making quick sketches
☐ **Coloured pens:** useful to distinguish between different types of measurements; red and black are a good contrast
☐ **Compass:** so that you can easily determine the north
☐ **Spirit level and set square:** useful for making sure that your measurements are taken on true horizontal and vertical lines
☐ **Camera:** useful for recording particular features, such as fireplaces, but you must ask the clients' permission before you use it

THE MEASURE SURVEY

First, make a plan of the room on graph paper. Although this will not be to finished standard, try to keep it as accurate as possible. Leave sufficient space around the plan to put in the actual measurements, and make sure you include fitted furniture, doors, cupboard doors and window swings or openings. Mark in all the services,

▶ *Look at this example of a survey sketch of the floor plan of a Victorian dining room. You will see not only the measurements for the length and width of the room but also all the individual measurements, such as the width and height of the windows, the sill height, the width of the doorways and size of the doors.*

KEY

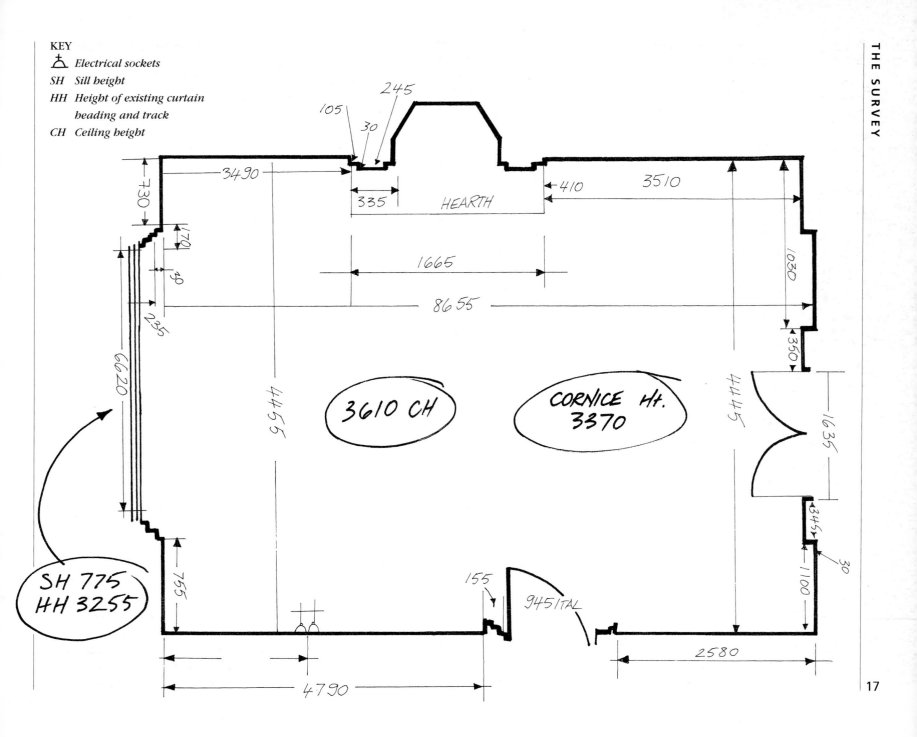

- ⚡ Electrical sockets
- **SH** Sill height
- **HH** Height of existing curtain heading and track
- **CH** Ceiling height

245

105

30

335

HEARTH

410

3510

3490

730

170

30

235

1665

1030

8655

6620

4455

350

3610 CH

CORNICE Ht. 3370

5445

1635

345

755

1100

30

SH 775
HH 3255

155

945 ITAL

2580

4790

including the position of all pipes, electrical sockets and radiators. Note the north point and any extreme measurements, such as a low ceiling that restricts headroom.

TAKING THE MEASUREMENTS

To take the measurements, start from the door and work clockwise around the room. Take the overall measurements, adding on the skirting depths. Make sure that you keep the tape completely taut while you are measuring so that the dimensions are absolutely accurate. For this reason, it is very much easier to work with a partner when you are measuring a very large space.

The next stage is to take all the individual measurements. Working on one wall at a time, take, for example, measurements of corner to fireplace, the height of the fireplace and all doors and windows. You must measure every detail, including dados, cornices, panels, height of window-sill to floor, and depth and width of sill. You will need all these details to produce an accurate working plan. You may find that you have to make further, larger scale rough plans in order to accommodate all these detailed measurements. For extra clarity, it is useful to use different colours – for example, put the measurements of the details in red and the overall dimensions in black.

When you have completed this part of the survey, measure the height of the room and the diagonals across the walls and floors. Finally, before you leave, take

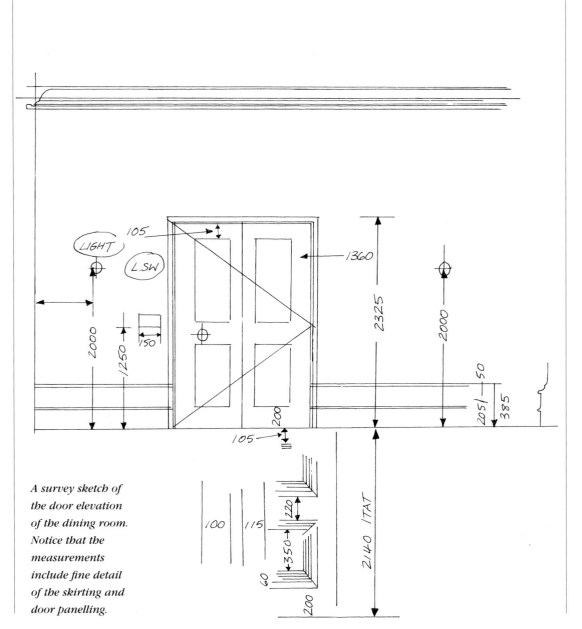

A survey sketch of the door elevation of the dining room. Notice that the measurements include fine detail of the skirting and door panelling.

photographs of the four elevations or make quick sketches of any notable features you feel should be recorded. It is relatively rare that you get *carte blanche* with a project to supply everything new. It is much more likely that you will need to incorporate some existing, and sometimes not very attractive, possessions into the scheme. It makes sense to measure and photograph these for easy reference when you are planning the layouts. Memory often plays tricks and does not always retain things satisfactorily, so try to start drawing up your plans as soon as possible after the survey.

Of course, if the project involved the whole house, you would need to survey each room or area individually.

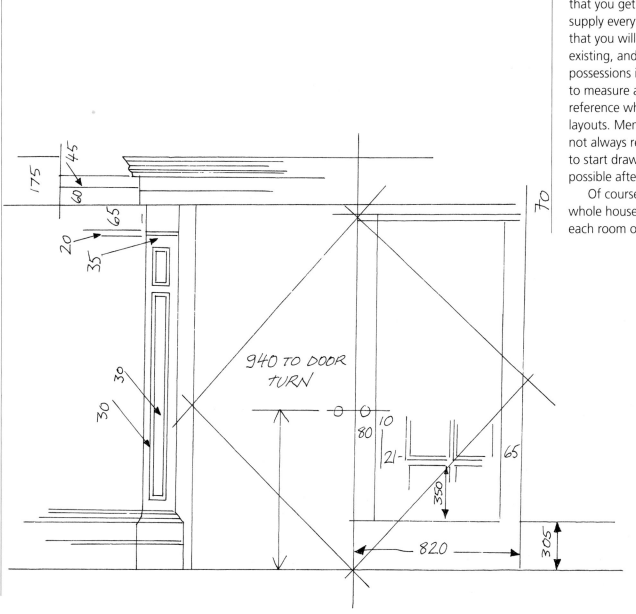

940 TO DOOR
TURN

A survey sketch of the internal doors elevation of the dining room showing the pillars with moulding on the architrave and the glazing panels on the doors. The measurements of all features in the room should be included so that they can later be transferred to your finished scale drawings.

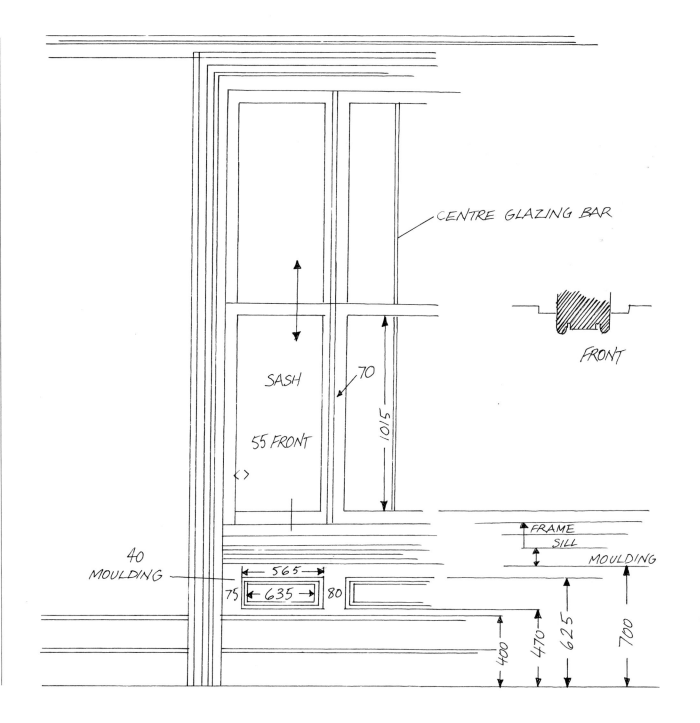

CENTRE GLAZING BAR

FRONT

SASH

70

1015

55 FRONT

⟨ ⟩

40
MOULDING

565

75 635 80

FRAME
SILL

MOULDING

400 470 625 700

A survey sketch of the window elevation of the dining room showing the precise measurements of the sashes, sill and mouldings. This elevation will be particularly useful when you come to work on the treatments for the curtains or blinds.

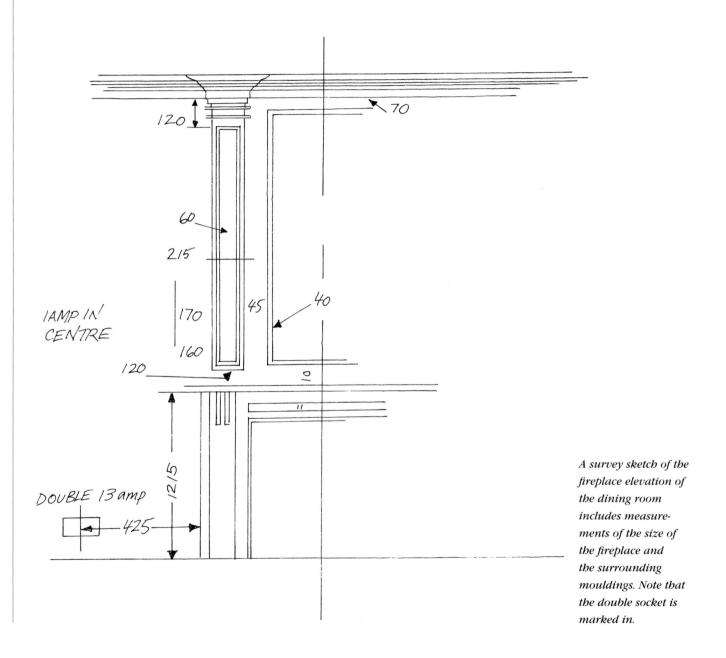

120

70

60

215

IAMP IN
CENTRE

170

45

40

160

120

10

11

12/5

DOUBLE 13 amp

425

*A survey sketch of the
fireplace elevation of
the dining room
includes measure-
ments of the size of
the fireplace and
the surrounding
mouldings. Note that
the double socket is
marked in.*

21

CHAPTER THREE

DRAWING UP PLANS

The plan is the most important drawing for the designer. It gives an overall view of the arrangements and dimensions of a given area, and, when it is combined with the analysis of space and the briefing notes, it provides the designer with a basis from which to work out a design solution.

Once the plan has been drawn up in rough you can begin to picture how a room might be laid out and this, in turn, can stimulate creative ideas.

The first working floor plan you draw up will give you the framework on which to try out different layouts until you come up with the best solution for the clients' needs. This will then be refined into a presentation plan, with a furniture layout, to present to the clients. The plan functions as a horizontal slice through a designed area at approximately 1 metre (3 ft) above floor level, and it is the basis for the whole design process.

Wall elevations, which are drawn to scale, relate to all the items on a flat wall. An elevation is usually drawn up from a plan, and no thicknesses are shown. You would show the shape of an adjacent cornice and skirting, but would not include the returns or adjacent windows or walls.

A section is a cross view on the vertical, which gives a view of the interior and exterior at the same time. The section uses the same plane as an elevation and is drawn up from a plan. Its position must be marked on the plan itself – e.g., A-A, B-B, C-C.

A plan with a furniture layout and elevations showing details, such as bookcases or window treatments, are the most useful forms of presentation to the clients. Carefully titled and mounted, they can be shaded or rendered to make them look more attractive and to give the clients a better idea of how the room will look.

▼ *An elevation showing a flat view of a bathroom wall.*

A section - that is, a cut through - view of the same bathroom wall, showing the side of the bath and inside the cupboard. ▼

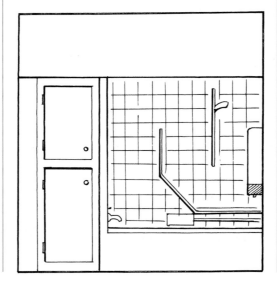

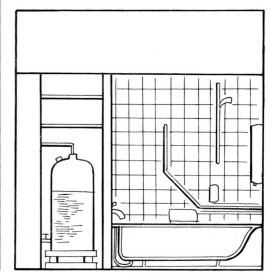

Remember that an elevation shows virtually no depth, so if you want to indicate one or two pieces of furniture in front of a wall – a wing chair at an angle, for example – a section would be preferable.

There are various types of plan, but you should draw a floor plan for your survey sketch. There are also site plans, which are used to show a site in its surrounding area; these are usually taken from ordnance survey maps. A site plan shows the overall site, its outbuildings and major features, and its access to the public highways. You will need to prepare a site plan only for a substantial project where a number of buildings are involved. Lighting and electrical plans are also important to the interior designer. These are described in Chapter 4, after the furniture layout.

A floor plan of a theatre showing the different areas. Thicker lines are used to indicate the external walls.

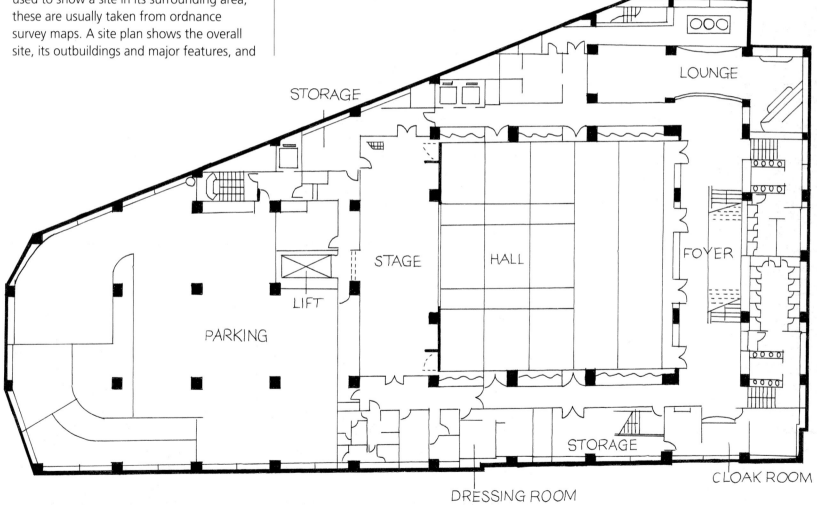

STORAGE

LOUNGE

STAGE

HALL

FOYER

LIFT

PARKING

STORAGE

CLOAK ROOM

DRESSING ROOM

23

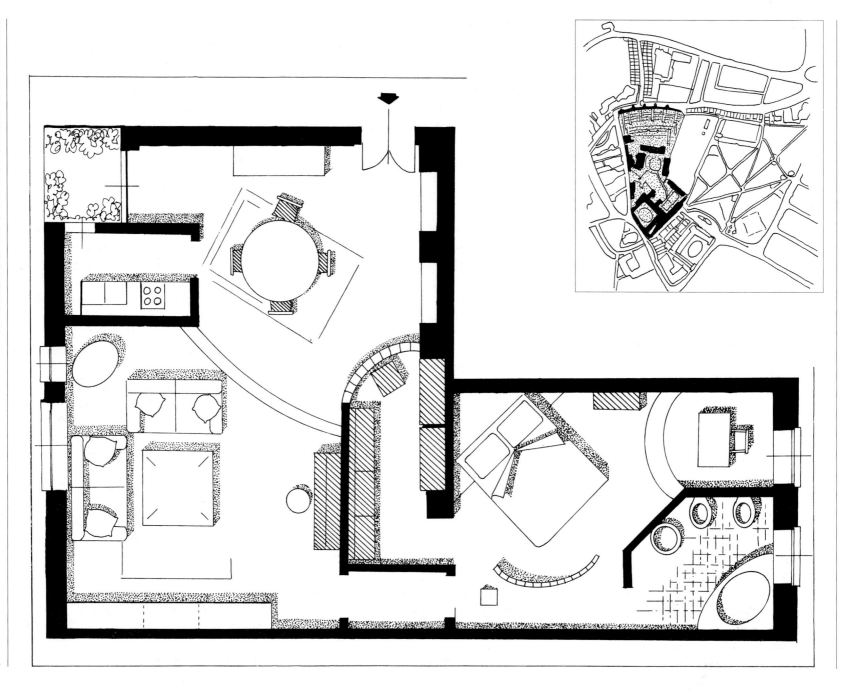

DRAWING A FLOOR PLAN, SECTIONS AND ELEVATIONS

EQUIPMENT

'A bad workman blames his tools', and for design work, good-quality, well-maintained equipment will certainly help avoid mistakes and frustrations. You will need the following equipment to draw accurate floor plans, sections and elevations:

☐ **Drawing board:** A1 (841 × 597mm/33 × 23½in) or A2 (597 × 419mm/23½ × 16½in) with parallel motion; the parallel bar, which replaces the T-square, moves smoothly up and down the drawing surface on a system of pulleys and cables.

☐ **Set square:** these come in various sizes – 45°, 30° or 60° – but an adjustable version is ideal and enables you to draw angled lines.

☐ **Eraser:** these do not, in general, work well on paper surfaces. When you remove pencil lines, India rubber gets grubby quickly and marks the paper and although plastic rubbers stay cleaner, they tend to crumble which, in turn, can cause smudging. Kneaded or putty erasers are probably best, because they are cleaner and can be moulded into shapes to correct even tiny errors. Plastic erasers are impregnated with a solvent, which dissolves ink, and you could try these for removing a small inked error, although you may well have to resort to a scalpel or razor blade to remove it completely.

☐ **Scalpel or razor blade:** for scratching out inked mistakes.

☐ **Clutch lead holder:** designed for drafting, this is really a pencil without a casing. The lead is contained in a plastic or metal barrel with a push-button mechanism that allows the lead to be extended as it is used and worn down. A special sharpener is usually incorporated into the removable button, and leads are available in a range of hardness. You can also buy fine clutch pencils which do not need sharpening.

A drafting pencil must always have a good sharp point.

☐ **Scale rule:** choose one with 1:20, 1:50, 1:10 and 1:100 scales.

☐ **Ruler:** you will need a plastic ruler at least 45cm (18in) long.

☐ **Circle templates:** these stencils are useful for drawing door and window swings.

☐ **Drawing pens**

PAPER

When you first draw up a plan and start the design process, you are making what are known as working drawings. At this stage, you do not want to waste money unnecessarily, and so you should work with thin detail, layout or tracing paper and save the better quality paper for your presentation drawings.

☐ **Tracing paper:** you should keep a number of different weights in your office, but 600 gsm would be adequate while you are working up a design. The most useful sizes are A1 (841 × 597mm/33 × 23½in) or A2 597 × 419mm/23½ × 16½in).

☐ **Detail paper:** this is similar to tracing paper, but is slightly more opaque. It is good for copying and tracing and for working out difficult ideas or details for a scheme so that you can overlay them on to a plan.

☐ **Layout paper:** this brilliant white, translucent paper can be used instead of detail or tracing paper when you want to use markers, pens and brushes. Its surface is more suitable for these media than detail or tracing paper. It is a versatile type of paper.

◀ *A plan showing the disposition of the furniture. Shading has been used to give depth and interest.*

◀ *(Inset) A site plan of a school, showing not only the layout of the buildings but also the main features in relation to the surrounding area.*

Desk-top drawing boards may have attached parallel motion, or you can use a T-square.

Some drawing boards are available on their own stands and with attached parallel motion.

This sophisticated type of free-standing drawing board is called a drafting machine.

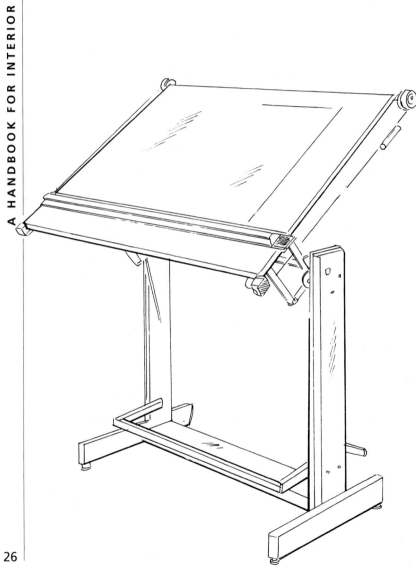

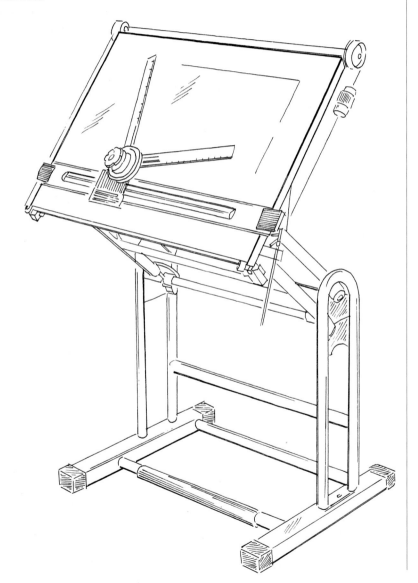

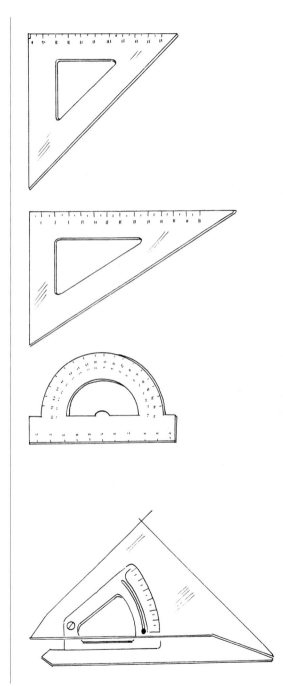

◄ *You will need a selection of set squares in various sizes to enable you to draw angles accurately. In addition to a 45° set square and one that has 30° and 60° angles, you will need a protractor to help you draw curved lines. An adjustable set square allows you to draw a range of angles.*

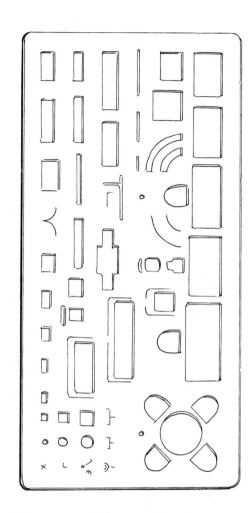

◄ *Curves are useful when you have to draw curved lines on plans.*

▲ *Furniture templates are available in different scales for drawing appropriate shapes on a floor plan to prepare the furniture layout.*

27

A floor plan showing the layout of the ground floor of a town house.

PLAN

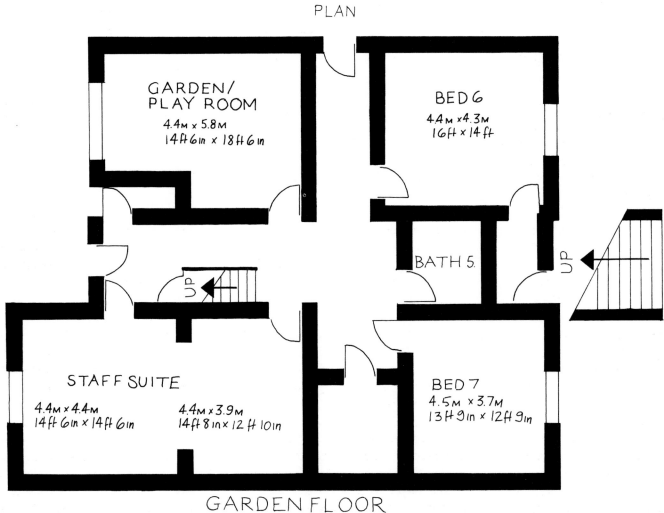

GARDEN/
PLAY ROOM
4.4м x 5.8м
14ft 6in x 18ft 6in

BED 6
4.4м x 4.3м
16ft x 14ft

BATH 5.

UP

UP

STAFF SUITE

4.4м x 4.4м
14ft 6in x 14ft 6in

4.4м x 3.9м
14ft 8in x 12ft 10in

BED 7
4.5м x 3.7м
13ft 9in x 12ft 9in

GARDEN FLOOR

DRAWING UP A PLAN

Before you start to draw, set your drawing board at a comfortable angle and make sure it is well lit and that no shadows are falling across it. Use a piece of layout paper as a backing sheet and fix this to the board with masking tape. Position and secure your chosen sheet of tracing or layout paper on top of this.

Before you put pencil to paper, decide on the scale of your drawing. Check that the overall dimensions will fit comfortably on your intended sheet size and will leave adequate space for the title panel. Try to find a scale that will allow you to include all the necessary details without having to draw up a huge plan. Use your clutch lead pencil, or an ordinary HB pencil, and the parallel bar to draw in the outline of the room from the measurements on your sketch survey, calculating the adjusted dimensions from your scale rule. Check the thickness of the walls as well as their length. Place the outline centrally on the sheet, and if it does not fit comfortably on the size of sheet you have chosen, start again at a smaller scale. If the drawing looks lost on the sheet or is too cramped, you could either change the size of sheet or reduce or enlarge the scale you are working in. Keep referring back to the sketch survey.

Remember that windows do not follow the same line as the walls and should be inset. Casement windows open, and you should show the swing of the opening section. Doors and their swings should also be included and, depending on the scale,

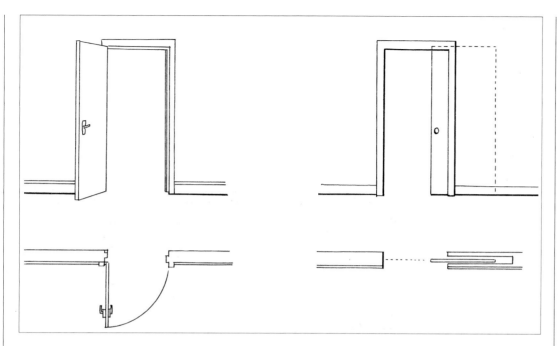

their thicknesses and the thicknesses of the architrave need to be indicated. Tick off each dimension as you draw it up.

You should now have a basic plan from which to start to evolve your design ideas. The plan is the framework on which you work out the layout of the space and the best way of using the space for the client's needs.

Everyone has their own way of working at this stage, but sketching your ideas on an overlay of tracing, detail or layout paper is a good way to begin. For this reason you must make sure when you draw the base plan that it is clear enough to read through an overlay. If it becomes evident that any of the original survey dimensions are inaccurate, arrange to return to the site to re-check this

▲ The left-hand illustration shows how to draw a standard door opening on a plan.

On the right-hand ▲ side is the way one form of sliding door should be drawn.

rather than muddling through and hoping for the best. Keep all your notes and reference material. Some of the dimensions you took at survey, for example, will not be required until you come to work on the presentation drawings.

The first plan is usually fairly messy and difficult to read, so it is a good idea to use an overlay and to trace over the original version, preferably in ink, so that it is easier to use for subsequent overlays. In the bottom right-hand corner put in the north

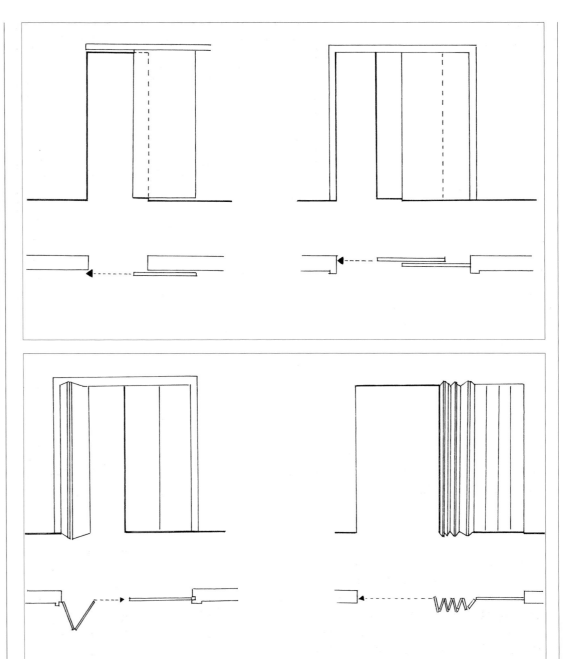

point, the scale of the drawing, the date of the drawing, the job number (every job should be allocated a number, and all related drawings, presentation or paperwork should carry this number), the address that relates to your drawing and your name. On presentation drawings this will become a full title panel, which will be discussed in Chapter 8.

ELEVATIONS AND SECTIONS

Details of vertical aspects of the design are shown on elevations and sections. The number of each that you present to the clients will depend on the amount of detail you need to include to explain the scheme as clearly as possible, and you will sometimes want to show all four walls. The elevations and sections also allow you to adjust proportions that do not seem to be working and to adjust the positions of details such as mirrors, cornices and dado rails. If there is a great deal of detail, it is possible to use a larger scale than the plan, but in this case you should place the elevations or sections on a separate sheet. Otherwise, you would probably place the elevations or sections above the plan on

◀ (Top) *Two other types of sliding door and how they should be drawn on a plan.*

◀ (Bottom) *How to draw folding doors on a plan.*

the same sheet, and you should bear this in mind when you are deciding on the scale and position of the actual plan on the sheet.

Elevations

Elevations show a flat view of a wall, with any detail on that wall such as bookshelves or a fireplace, but they do not show furniture that is to be placed in front of the wall. To draw an elevation, place overlay paper onto the base plan. Plot the walls by drawing pencil lines that extend from the plan, using the parallel bar or set square to make sure they are parallel. Use the vertical measurements from the survey to plot the height of the wall and the dimensions of elements such as the window-sill or fireplace. When all the details have been finished, which is usually after the furniture layout has been completed, the drawing will be transferred to paper suitable for presentation, inked in and titled.

Sections

Sections are normally used to illustrate two or more separate areas that are divided by walls to show how they relate to each other. They would also include an area of up to 1 metre (3 ft) in front of the wall, so some furniture, shown to scale, might be included. The area shown in the section should be marked on the actual plan in a broken line, and this and the sections themselves labelled A-A, B-B and so on.

Sections are drawn in the same way as elevations – that is, by extending the plan in pencil on an overlay with the parallel bar

Examples of a
window elevation

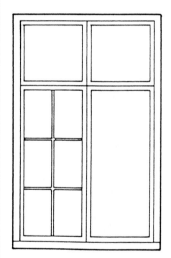

and calculating the length of the lines from the vertical dimensions on your survey sketch. Again, this drawing would normally be completed after the furniture layout has been decided, and it would then be transferred to presentation paper, inked in and titled.

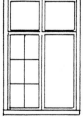

TRANSFERRING DRAWINGS TO PRESENTATION PAPER

Presenting drawings on tracing or overlay paper does not look professional. Therefore, when you have completed a plan, you might want to have a copy made. Dyeline copies can be made onto good-quality paper, and it is not an expensive process, although it can result in a dark background. When there is not too much fine or soft detail involved, plans can also be copied onto plain paper. This is expensive, but the results are good. If you are going to render your plans, sections or elevations, you will need to copy them onto watercolour paper. This can be done by photocopying on a large commercial photocopier that will take a paper as thick as watercolour paper or by back-tracing. To back-trace, turn your drawing over and use a 2B pencil to go over the drawing on the underside of the paper. Put the paper, right side up, over the watercolour paper and hold it in place with masking tape. Carefully re-trace the drawing onto the paper. Your hands will get dirty as you do this, so take care to avoid smudging.

If you decide that structural alterations are needed, you must show the client how these changes will affect the property. One way of doing this is to show them a plan of the existing building with the structural changes drawn in in red. It is extremely unwise to press ahead with anything but the most minor alterations without first enlisting the advice of an architect or without a structural surveyor's report. The safety of your client is your responsibility.

A plan and elevations on the same sheet provide a neat, organized way of presenting your planning ideas to the client.

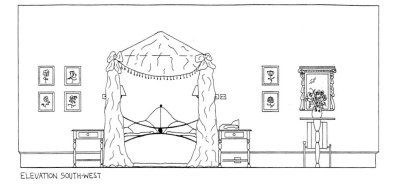

ELEVATION SOUTH-WEST

PLAN

INKING IN

When you ink in the plans, sections and elevations, complete the entire drawing using a 0.25 pen. When the drawing is complete, make the walls stronger by going over the outlines with a 0.50 pen to make the plan bolder and easier to read.

When you have finished drawing, always clean your drawing board, scale rulers and so on with warm, soapy water. Use lighter fuel to remove any stubborn marks, but remember to use this in a well-ventilated area and do not smoke or have a naked flame in the same room because it is highly flammable. If you take care of your equipment it will last longer and will help you to maintain a high standard of work.

Correcting an ink drawing

Plastic erasers are impregnated with a solvent that dissolves ink, and you should try to remove the error with one of these before using a scraping technique. However, undoubtedly the most efficient way of removing a persistent error is to use either a razor blade or scalpel. Point the blade in the opposite direction from the way it is being scraped, and when the error has been removed, smooth over the area with a soft eraser.

A plan with sections. Note the way in which the sections are related to the plan.

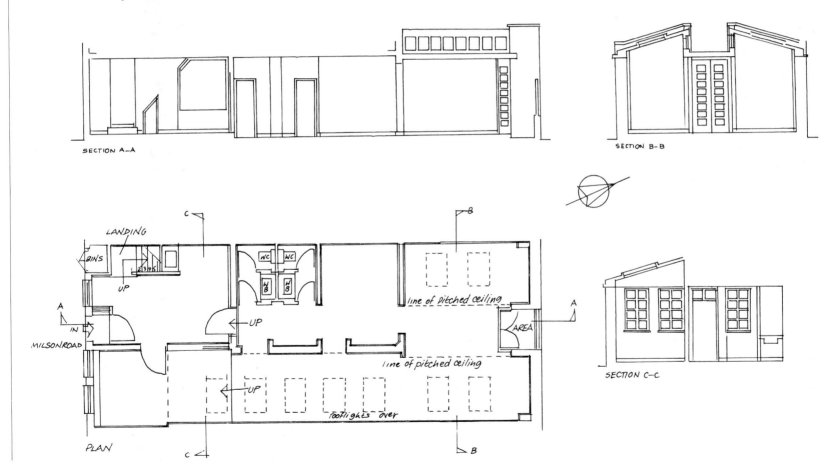

SECTION A–A

SECTION B–B

SECTION C–C

LANDING

BINS

UP

WC WC

line of pitched ceiling

AREA

line of pitched ceiling

IN

WILSON ROAD

UP

UP

footlights over

PLAN

CHAPTER FOUR

PLANNING THE SPACE

Now that you have a base plan to work with, a good idea of the clients' requirements and your own design analysis, you can set about planning the way in which space will be used. Your aims are to make the space not only practical and workable but also aesthetically pleasing.

Apart from the practical considerations involved in developing a scheme, you will, of course, need inspiration. This can be a colour or a combination of colours, perhaps in a picture or rug, or it might be an unusually textured material or some graphics. An architectural style, a theme, a fictional character or even a contemporary personality could provide a starting point, and it is something to keep in the back of your mind throughout the planning stage.

A tight budget can in itself be an inspiration, as it provides a challenge to find appropriate and inexpensive materials and calls for imagination and inventiveness.

In budgeting for any project, it is important to prioritize the spending and to allocate a reasonable part of that budget to thorough preparation. Clients do not always appreciate that these 'hidden' costs are an important investment and that a good framework will allow their furniture

It is important to establish the mood or style the client would prefer to live with. Here, a modern style emphasizes space and light.

and possessions to be shown and displayed to much greater effect.

Sometimes you will be required to work in a consultancy capacity only, rather than designing a whole scheme. It is possible that all the structural work will have been done before you are contacted, and the clients feel they cannot achieve the decorative style they have in mind without professional help. Many jobs involve recycling clients' existing possessions, improving seating arrangements to provide good conversation areas and rearranging pictures and accessories to give more impact.

THE DESIGN SOLUTION

A large part of design work involves problem solving and decision making. Sometimes you will arrive at this quickly, perhaps from instinct or by drawing on experience. At other times, however, it is helpful to go through what are really four essential phases of the design process:

☐ Gathering all relevant information, thoroughly analysing the priorities, requirements and constraints – that is, taking the brief, completing the design analysis and carrying out the research.
☐ Producing ideas and concepts – that is, working up possible schemes from your basic plan.
☐ Looking at the alternatives and deciding on the best solution; there are nearly always several possible designs.
☐ Implementing the chosen solution.

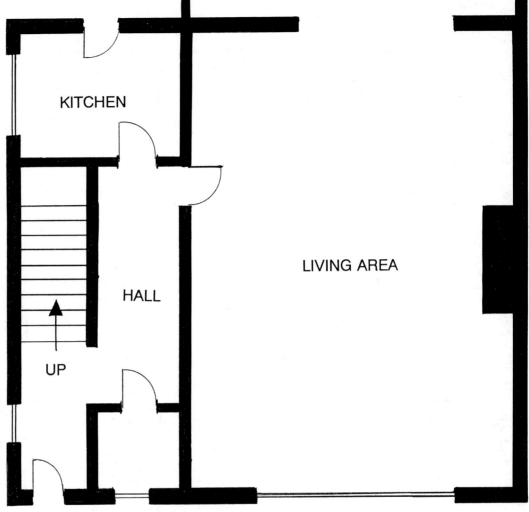

This process is often referred to as design methodology, which really means nothing more than planning actions in chronological order and approaching the whole design process in a structured and systematic way. Design methodology began in the 1960s, although the advent of computer-aided design (CAD) confused its progress

Good planning starts with an accurate scale plan of the area. The furniture can be shown with templates in the same scale.

somewhat. While CAD can take over the routine work of drawing and processing information, it is important to remember that it cannot 'design' as such. There is no doubt, however, that designers will come to rely increasingly on computers and that they will eventually take a great deal of the repetition out of the work. There are already computers that not only show variations on the layout of a space at the touch of a button but that can even show the same space in a variety of different colour schemes. The advent of virtual reality will one day enable interior designers to recreate detailed views of period interiors so that they can be refurbished with the greatest accuracy.

Methodology is now well established, but although it can help the designer reach an intelligent and workable solution, it can never replace creativity. It is a useful control on projects of all sizes but is particularly valuable when you are dealing with larger, more complex briefs. Although it sounds rather mundane, when you are working under pressure – which is certainly the case with most design work – methodology provides a useful framework from which you can tackle a project.

If you are planning a whole house or flat, give careful consideration to the clients' lifestyle. Do they really need a dining room, for example, or would the space be better used as a playroom or as a dual-purpose space such as a study-cum-dining room? Would it be sensible to create a separate room for teenagers? Is the entrance to the property in the most practical place? You

must try to make sure that the space works for your clients and without careful planning you could end up with dead, cramped or awkward corners that will cause daily irritation.

As designer you must also be aware of the practical aspects of space. Access for large pieces of furniture can be a problem,

for instance, so you must check the widths of doors, look at the angles of stairs and the size of lifts if appropriate and bear these in mind when choosing furniture for the project. Huge problems will ensue if any item cannot be installed.

As we have already noted, the clients' safety is always the responsibility of the

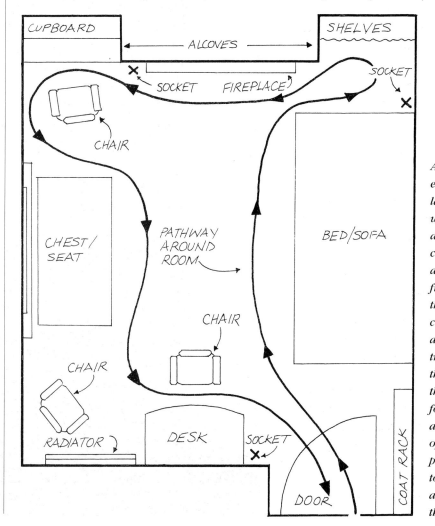

A useful way of establishing that a layout is working well and that there is ample room for circulation is to draw an overlay of the furniture layout and then to draw in curved lines with arrows indicating the traffic flow around the room. Remember that you must allow for doors, windows and drawers to be opened and that people must be able to move easily around and between the furniture.

designer. Although the rules and regulations on domestic safety are not very carefully defined, you must keep this aspect in mind throughout the planning stage. Do not, for example, specify a floor finish or an awkwardly placed rug that could be hazardous for very young or elderly members of a household. Encourage clients to install smoke detectors and fire alarms, to light stairways well, and to make certain all electrics comply with established safety standards.

If you are to plan successfully, you must know how much space people need to carry out a particular function. Buy a book that contains the necessary information and make sure that you understand what is involved. You should have a good grasp of constantly used dimensions, such as the height and depth of average work surfaces in kitchens – 600mm (23½ in) – desk heights – 720mm (28¼ in) – and the depth required for clothes on a hanger – 600mm (23½ in) – or the amount of space a person needs to pass between two pieces of furniture. Allow space for drawers and doors to be opened and closed easily without knocking into other pieces of furniture, and make sure that all the members of the household will be able to circulate around a room without obstruction. The comfort of your client is a prime concern, and because people tend to come in varying shapes and sizes, you should be prepared to adapt measurements accordingly.

Folding doors are a practical, simple way to gain maximum use of space in restricted areas.

Architectural detailing plays an important part in the successful use of space. Not only is it aesthetically pleasing, but it is also functional, giving a finished look and helping to protect the plasterwork or wallcovering. The proportions of a whole room can be altered by the positioning of dados and picture rails and by the depth of cornices or skirting boards. Moving or extending architectural details can offer all sorts of design opportunities, such as incorporating bookcases, providing a canopy above a bed, or fronting sloping ceilings with doors or curtains to provide extra storage space. Providing space for storage is an essential factor in planning. Few homes or offices have sufficient storage facilities. Look carefully at what needs to be stored, including items such as bed linen, suitcases, extra seating and garden furniture, and plan so that everything is comfortably housed with easy access. Use wall space, awkward corners or understairs areas to make extra storage space. Peninsular or island units under basins or window seats in recesses are excellent ways of maximizing the available space. Good storage both helps to remove unnecessary clutter and increases the amount of available workspace.

The services such as heating, plumbing and electricity and even air-conditioning systems should be taken into consideration right from the start of a project. The points of supply will certainly affect some of your planning decisions, and you must also give careful consideration to the position of ducts, pipes and radiators. These will sometimes already be installed, in which case your function will be to conceal and camouflage them.

The planning of kitchens and bathrooms requires special care and attention. Ideally, every kitchen should have what is referred to as the 'work triangle', which is the positioning of the sink, the oven and hob, and the food storage and preparation areas for maximum efficiency. This can sometimes be provided in a galley layout or with the addition of an island unit.

Bathrooms, one of the most frequently used rooms in the house, do not always seem to receive the creative input they deserve. Your aim should be to produce a room that is both comfortable and welcoming. When it comes to planning the bathroom, you must make sure that the basin is the right height for the user, and that there is sufficient space around the bath and shower to kneel and bathe a child in a family bathroom. Fortunately, there is a wide range of bathroom fitments to help you with your planning. Your choice of taps can dictate the style of the bathroom, and the basins are available with pedestals, which conceal the plumbing, or they can be wall hung, when the plumbing is concealed behind a partition wall. Counter-top basins are, as the name suggests, set in a hole in the counter. Bidets and baths, too, are available in a wide variety of shapes and sizes, with a choice of plugs or pop-up waste holes. There is also a choice of materials, of which cast iron, though heavy is still considered the most durable. WCs are available in varied shapes and sizes, many specifically designed to hide the plumbing,

and where space allows, it is best if a WC is in some form of recess if it is not in a separate room.

Structural alterations may be the only solution to making the most of a particular space, perhaps by resiting a door or by knocking two rooms into one or even through some form of extension. However, an imaginative approach to planning can maximize the use of the space and overcome the need for major structural work, and there are a number of accepted structural and decorative ways to increase the sense of space and height in a room. Mirrors can be used to open up a space, while partition walls can be removed to make one large room from two smaller ones. You may need to put in extra support for such a change, and you must seek the advice of an architect and structural surveyor for this work. A suspended ceiling can be put in if a ceiling is too high, and floor-to-ceiling cupboards can increase the feeling of space. Never undertake any radical structural alterations without thinking through very carefully what you are trying to achieve in spatial terms.

Another aspect of planning is the use of shape and form. Form can give a room an extra visual dimension, and contrasting shapes can make a room look more interesting – oval and circular shapes can be mixed with square, rectangular and oblong

The decorative border on the wall tiles gives a visual link between the bathroom and shower cubicle and the 'back to wall' fittings allow the unsightly pipework to be neatly hidden away.

ones, for example, or a curved seating unit can be placed in a square room, a curved bedhead on a blank wall or a circular mirror over a square fireplace. Add visual interest by varying the height of furniture in a room to break the monotony that results when everything is at one level. Try to create a focal point – a fireplace is an obvious example – and plan the seating around it. Remember to provide tables nearby so that cups or glasses can be placed on them comfortably. Whenever possible, devise built-in storage or provide suitable free-standing furniture so that some of the clutter and unsightly wires from televisions and music systems are hidden from view.

Try to avoid placing the furniture in a confrontational way in a layout. It is unwelcoming to be immediately confronted with the side of a bed or the back of a sofa as you enter a room. Of course, a layout must be aesthetically pleasing, but if the positioning of the furniture is not thought through in detail, the room will not work.

◀ In a sitting room it is important to create comfortable conversation areas and flexible furniture arrangements so that a conversation group can be easily enlarged. Before planning a layout, discuss how the room will be

used, how many people will need to be seated and how the client likes to entertain.

▶ Buying or commissioning furniture can be an important part of the interior designer's work.

THE FURNITURE LAYOUT

A furniture layout cannot be a hit and miss affair. You must check that the furniture you would like to use – whether this is some of the clients' existing furniture or new items you have selected – will fit comfortably within the room. To do this, draw the furniture to scale on layout paper, either by measuring the actual pieces or by taking the dimensions from a catalogue, and cut these out into templates. Move the templates around the plan until you have a satisfactory working arrangement.

Although you can buy furniture templates in the form of stencils, these may not provide exactly what you need, and if you do decide to use the stencils, make certain that you select one that is in the same scale as the base plan.

If you find it hard to envisage the space, you can always make a paper model. Redraw the plan and all four elevations on fairly stiff paper and cut them out. Then glue

or staple the elevations to the sides of the plan. This is a particularly useful exercise when there are different ceiling heights within a room and you are trying to select the best walls for built-in cupboards or bookshelves. Look out, too, for varying floor levels, which could affect your design.

When you have finalized the furniture layout, back-trace the plan onto thick layout paper. To back-trace turn your drawing over and, using a 2B pencil, repeat the drawing on the underside of the paper. Then place it right side up onto the layout paper and hold it in place with masking tape. Re-trace the drawing onto the paper and draw in the furniture in pencil using the templates. When you are inking-in, complete the entire drawing using a 0.25 pen and then make the walls straight by going over the outline with a 0.50 pen.

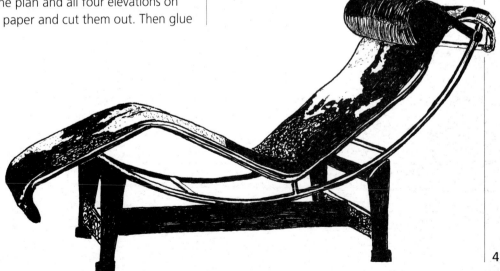

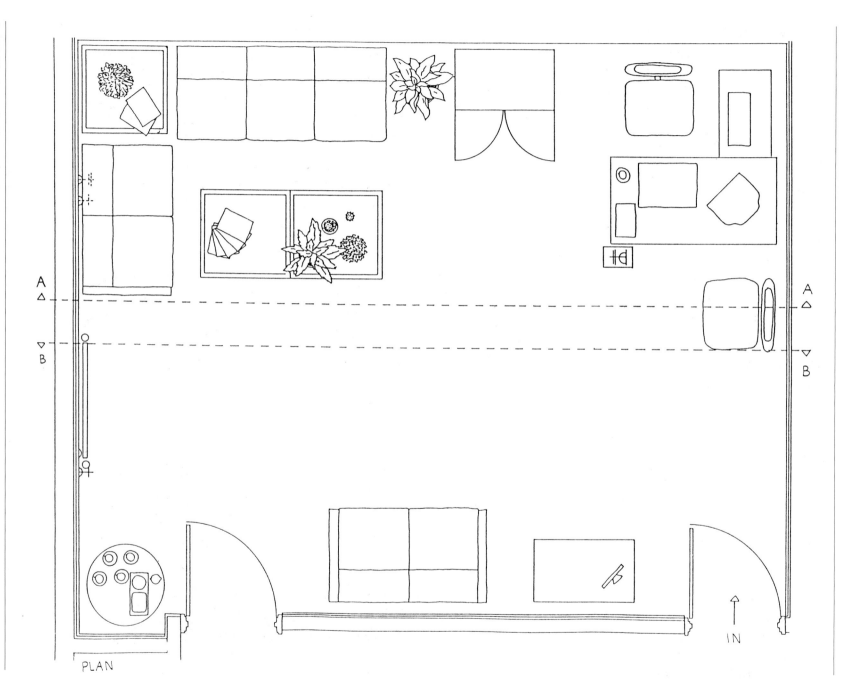

A   A
△   △

B   B
▽   ▽

PLAN

IN

LIGHTING PLANS

Once you have decided on the furniture layout you can consider the best way of lighting the space. All too often lighting is treated like a decorative accessory, which is added at the last moment. When you start to consider a lighting scheme, you may find it helpful to think it through under three different categories, which together go to make up a full lighting scheme.

General lighting

General lighting is intended to achieve a good all round level of light. For this you could use table lamps and standard lamps, pendants, wall lights, wall-mounted up-lighters and recessed down-lighters or wall washers on mains or low voltage.

All these fittings are more effective, efficient and flexible if they are combined with a dimming system.

Task lighting

This is used to light specific functions within a space. Among the options to be considered are fluorescent lights; low-voltage desk lamps; adjustable, recessed low-voltage down-lighters; powerful up-lighters, bouncing light off the ceiling to light a whole working area; and spotlights on tracks.

◀ *An example of a furniture layout which has been created by using furniture templates.*

▶ *Examples of different kinds of standard and low-voltage down-lighters.*

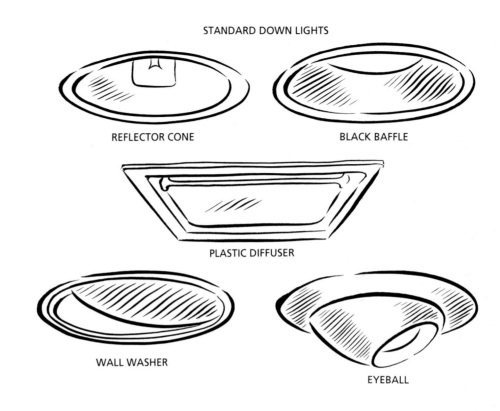

STANDARD DOWN LIGHTS

REFLECTOR CONE

BLACK BAFFLE

PLASTIC DIFFUSER

WALL WASHER

EYEBALL

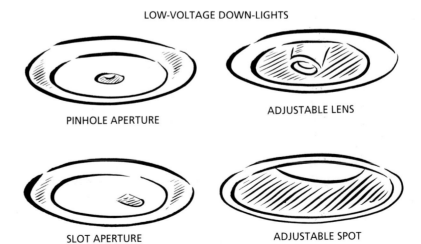

LOW-VOLTAGE DOWN-LIGHTS

PINHOLE APERTURE

ADJUSTABLE LENS

SLOT APERTURE

ADJUSTABLE SPOT

It is very important to position light fittings carefully if they are to be of any use. Relate them to the positions of furniture and equipment on your furniture layout.

(a) High lamps cast shadows.

(b) A desk or working area is well lit with a concealed light.

(c) A light behind the head is good for reading.

(e) A naked bulb gives glare.

(f) A rise and fall fitting will help eliminate glare.

(g) A long table may need two lights.

(d) A centre light tends to cast shadows.

(b) It is helpful to provide lighting inside cupboards.

Accent or display lighting

Lighting can also be used to add interest and drama by lighting pictures and decorative objects. Track lighting, adjustable down-lighters, up-lighters, picture lights and framing projectors will all achieve this. The advantages of low-voltage lighting are that they have a more tightly controlled beam and more discreet fittings, generate less heat, are more economic and efficient to use and give excellent colour rendering. They do, however, need a special inductive dimmer, and will sometimes have a separate transformer that will need to be housed.

Safety lighting

Particular attention must be given to lighting on stairs or in areas of general assembly. In public areas a battery-operated back-up system should be provided.

The purpose of the bulb

Flexibility is the key to the most effective lighting, and for this you need control. The source of control in any lighting scheme is the bulb, confusingly referred to professionally as a 'lamp'.

The best known is the incandescent bulb, which gives off a warm, inviting light and is available in various strengths and colours. Fluorescent bulbs or tubes are durable and inexpensive to run, but the quality of the light can be cold and harsh and it needs some form of diffusion. There are some new compact ranges, which can be used in decorative wall or ceiling lights or even in table lamps. Tungsten halogen produces a crisp, white light, which is very suitable for indirect or exterior lighting.

There is a wide variety of spot lights available for use with mains voltage or with low-energy, light-efficient, low-voltage bulbs. Low voltage gives very accurate control of the light beam, and crown or internally silvered lamps give an even more precise control. Dimmer switches offer flexible control.

Choosing fixtures

Fixtures on display in a store often look smaller than they will in a room. Before making a final selection, therefore, you should check the measurements carefully on site. Many fittings are available in graded sizes, so you can specify the appropriate size. When you are preparing a lighting plan consider how a fitting will direct light and whether it will put the light where you want it. Purchase and operating costs will, of course, be a factor, and if a fixture is likely to be in use for several hours at a time, you might want to consider a low-energy unit, because although the initial outlay might be greater, it would be more economical in the long run.

☐ **Down-lighters:** can be recessed in the ceiling or surface-mounted, and they can be mains or low-voltage. They can also be directional, so they can be angled exactly where the light is required.

☐ **Wall washers:** are a form of down-lighter that 'washes' the wall with a glow of light. They can also be adjusted to highlight objects on the wall.

▶ Decorative table lamps: *an art nouveau Tiffany-style lamp, with a coloured stained glass shade on a metal base, and an art deco table lamp, with a draped female figure as the base and a globe shade. A brass oil lamp can have either a frosted or a clear glass shade; the modern lamp has a more streamlined appearance.*

▶ Floor lamps: *a tall up-lighter bounces light off the ceiling; small up-lighters can be used to highlight individual plants or objects or to flood a wall with light; the traditional-style standard lamp, which is good for reading when it is placed next to a chair, can be used with a variety of shades; modern standard lamps are usually adjustable.*

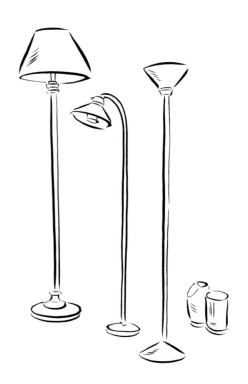

◀ Desk or task lamps: *an adjustable angled work lamp; an adjustable spot light; a traditional desk lamp; a modern desk lamp, which will take cool, fluorescent bulbs.*

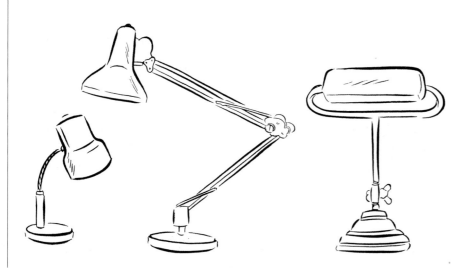

□ **Up-lighters:** can be floor- or wall-mounted, or they can be a version of the traditional standard lamp. To give general lighting, an up-lighter needs to bounce light off the ceiling so the fitting you choose, whether freestanding or wall mounted, needs to be high enough to achieve this.

□ **Spot lights:** can be mounted directly on the wall or on a track, and then be angled towards surfaces or objects where light is required. Framing projectors and mini-tracks, which are scaled-down systems for display shelves and the like, are an effective way of lighting works of art.

□ **Table and standard lamps:** can provide task lighting, or they can be used as general lighting, when they give a pleasant background glow. Standard lamps used to have a poor design image, but these days they are available in a variety of pleasing shapes and styles and they give particularly good reading light.

□ **Wall lights:** are usually traditional in appearance. They provide a soft background light.

□ **Pendants:** come in a variety of shapes and sizes, but they generally hang from the centre of the ceiling and give an unflattering and often inadequate light.

□ **Chandeliers:** are highly decorative, but they can be glaring and so work best with low-voltage bulbs.

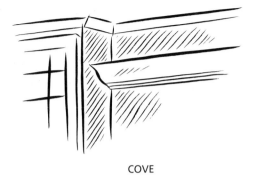

COVE

PELMET

CORNICE

WALL BRACKET

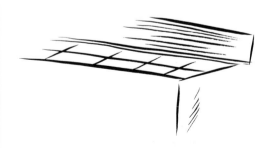

SOFFIT OR BAFFLE

Coves, cornices, pelmets and soffits or baffles can be used when indirect lighting is required. Simple and architectural in design, they ensure that light sources are hidden from view and prevent glare.

Coves spread light upwards onto the ceiling, while cornices spread light below. Used behind pelmets, they direct light up to the ceiling. Soffits or baffles prevent glare over work areas and can direct light to specific areas.

47

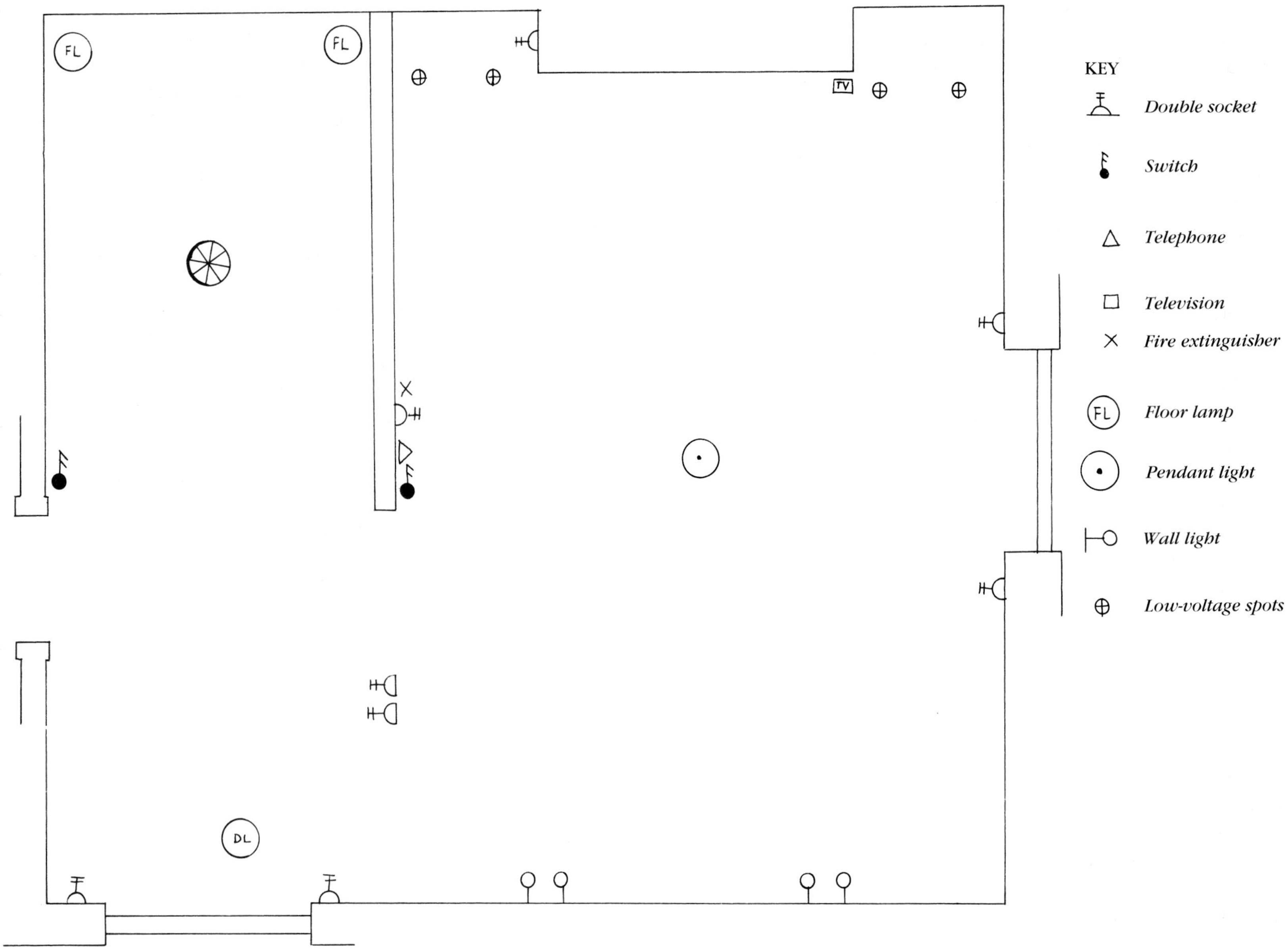

KEY

⌂   *Double socket*

♪   *Switch*

△   *Telephone*

☐   *Television*

✕   *Fire extinguisher*

FL   *Floor lamp*

⊙   *Pendant light*

⊢○   *Wall light*

⊕   *Low-voltage spots*

Before you decide on a lighting scheme you should consider the function of the room, the times of day it is used and the amount of natural light available. To achieve a good all-round level of light you need a system that will direct light both horizontally and vertically, and when you come to plan the decorative scheme you should bear in mind that light-coloured surfaces reflect light and so make it easier to achieve good lighting distribution than dark-coloured surfaces, which absorb it. In a dark panelled room, for example, the lighting will have to be increased to give a good level of light.

Drawing the lighting plan

The plan can be drawn as an overlay on tracing paper. Draw an outline of the room or rooms and then, using the appropriate symbols, mark in the electrical sockets, switches and fittings you suggest. The most commonly used symbols for lighting plans are shown opposite.

◀ A lighting plan can be shown on its own, as here, or it can be combined, as an overlay, with the furniture layout. Think carefully about the positions of sockets, to avoid trailing wires from lamps and appliances, and of switches, to give easy access. It is also important to give a clear key identifying the symbols you have used. Any additional instructions for the electrician can be shown in note form at the lower right-hand corner of the plan.

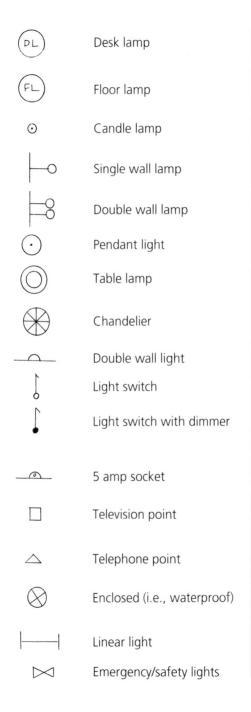

Use a pencil for your first attempt, and then, when you are certain you have a flexible, workable, well-balanced and interesting scheme, ink it in.

Use different coloured lines to identify the various circuits, and draw these from the fitments to each circuit and back to its switch so that you can see at a glance how the scheme will operate. Your circuits should all switch from near to the door and should give a flexible system. If, for example, there was one circuit for table lamps, another for ceiling-mounted or recessed fittings and a third for picture lights and other display lighting, it would be possible to create several different lighting effects during an evening.

Your plan could be presented as an overlay and attached over the furniture layout, held in place by pieces of velcro or Blu-tack, double-sided tape, or it could be photocopied onto plain white paper and presented as a separate plan.

CHAPTER FIVE

PUTTING TOGETHER A COLOUR SCHEME

Colour is probably both the most exciting and the least expensive decorative tool at your disposal. It is, of course, just one aspect of an interior scheme and would not normally be viewed in isolation, but you should be aware of the ways it can be used to create atmosphere and period style, and to play unusual tricks to alter the appearance of space.

With period interiors it is sometimes effective to work with the colours and patterns that were typical of the day.

Do not be afraid to experiment with colour and seek out different sources of inspiration. This is a rewarding area of the work, and one of the most pleasurable aspects of the commission.

Even from the earliest days colour has changed with the fashions. Colour was widely used in medieval and Renaissance times, the fourteenth to sixteenth centuries, when interior and exterior walls were often painted or stencilled and fabrics were used as wallcoverings, canopies, banners and room dividers. The natural, vegetable dyes would have made the colours strong and vibrant. The baroque style, prevalent in the seventeenth century, favoured rich shades, and rich, contrasting colours such as gold with bright blue or crimson with ivory were often used for effect. In the early to mid-eighteenth century delicate pastels were a feature of the rococo style, but the early Georgian period in England is often associated with 'drab' colours such as brown, olive or grey. Colours grew stronger and brighter during the eighteenth century. The neo-classical palette favoured in the late eighteenth century included green, lilac, pink and terracotta. There was also a cooler range of colours, such as pale grey, blue, green, white and gold, which were particularly popular in France.

Many American fashions were influenced by British styles, but the paint used had more sheen than the eggshell and matt paints of Georgian England, because the American pigments were mixed with milk. The preferred colours included yellow ochre,

American beaux-arts *interiors often drew on previous periods to create luxurious effects. Modern fittings were designed on period lines.*

51

blue-grey, ox-blood and deep blue-green, which was often teamed with burnt sienna.

By the end of the eighteenth century, the manufacture of ready mixed paints had begun with the production of flat, matt tones. The aspect of the room was now taken into consideration when choosing a colour scheme – cool colours were chosen for south-facing rooms and warmer tones for those facing north. The introduction of new synthetic pigments resulted in a much wider and more affordable range of colours. During the Regency period colours were vivid and daring – blues and golds, cherry red, saffron yellow and subtle turquoise – while in the early nineteenth century the dominant Empire and Federal colours were ruby, green, lemon yellow and azure blue, though a quieter palette was also fashionable. In the mid- to late nineteenth century colours were rich and opulent and included red, chocolate brown, Stuart green, Prussian blue, burgundy, magenta, black and gold.

In the late nineteenth century the Second Empire style in France is associated with orange, red, blue and pink. The Arts & Crafts movement in England favoured olive green, plum, hyacinth blue, burgundy, lemon yellow, taupe and rose, ivory, pale grey and white, and the American Victorian period in the mid- to late nineteenth century used a similar palette of colour. Art nouveau brought mauve pinks, greens, turquoise, blue and yellow into fashion, and by the early twentieth century art deco, with the colours of the sets and costumes of Diaghilev's Ballets Russes, was bringing orange, deep blue and black, red and gold

into fashion, often setting them against the neutral coloured walls that were advocated by the Bauhaus School. The 1920s were a period of glitter and gloss, and the Hollywood glamour of the 1930s made all-white rooms fashionable. Strong colours came back into fashion in the late 1940s and 1950s, perhaps in reaction to the austerities of war. These days the inspiration for colour in paints, wallpapers, floorcoverings and textiles comes from a mixture of sources, and individuality is the key.

THE COLOUR WHEEL

The colour wheel is invaluable when you are putting together a colour scheme. All the colours in the spectrum – red, orange, yellow, green, blue and violet – are included, but not the neutrals – black, white and grey. Red, blue and yellow are the pure primary colours, and the other colours are created from them. Secondary colours are made by mixing two primary colours together – for example, blue and yellow make green, red and blue make violet, and red and yellow make orange. If you then mix a primary colour with one of the secondary colours next to it, you have a tertiary colour.

The complete colour wheel would therefore read: red, red/orange, yellow, yellow/green, green, blue/green, violet, red/violet. These are the pure colours from which limitless shades, tints and tones can be obtained by adding black, white and grey. Colours opposite one another on the

wheel are called complementary colours. The colours on one side of the wheel are warm and advancing – that is, they appear to come towards you – and those on the other side are cool and receding.

PLANNING A COLOUR SCHEME

Your client may have strong colour preferences or dislikes, but before you make any decisions consider the aspect of the room. If it is a south-facing room, you may need a fairly cool palette; a north-facing room, on the other hand, will need warm colours to restore the balance. An eastern light would benefit from soft colours to diffuse the harshness. Next, look at the architectural style, which might influence your choice or at least suggest the degree of formality or informality that is required in the room. Colour also allows a certain amount of leeway: a room without colour must be virtually flawless if it is to succeed, but a little colour will distract from a multitude of sins. An all-white scheme can be very demanding to live with and can make anything less than perfect look rather unappealing. Colour can also be used to give a sense of cohesion throughout a house.

If the proportions of the room are unsatisfactory, colour can be used to improve the balance. A traditional way of 'opening out' small or dark rooms is to use light colours, but an alternative is to accept their limitations and to decorate them in rich or brilliant colours that compensate for lack

The plain white background provides the perfect foil for the light oak-veneered units. Black accessories have been used to give an effective accent colour and the crisp contemporary light fittings provide an up-to-date look. The black and white floor and blind continue the theme. Restraint with colour will often result in a scheme with as much impact as the use of a very colourful palette.

of space by becoming a feature in their own right. Dark, rich colours can provide a warm background against which books and decorative objects can glow.

A ceiling can appear lower if it is in a darker tone than the walls, especially if this colour is extended to the level of the picture rail. The floor should be covered so that it is in the same tonal value. Breaking up the wall with a dado rail also brings the eye down, as does the addition of a deep decorative border at or just below cornice level. In a low-ceilinged room, the ceiling should be lighter than or a similar colour to the walls, or it should be painted to match the background of the wallpaper.

In general, light tones recede and dark tones advance into a room. A long, narrow room or a corridor can appear to be foreshortened if the end wall is decorated in a dark colour, and the space can be made to look even wider if the skirting matches the floor.

Disguise ugly features in a room by colouring them so that they recede into their background. Use the alternative technique to make an attractive piece of furniture or an architectural feature stand out against a contrasting background, and you could take this a stage further by outlining them with a border.

A white Shaker-style kitchen provides a calm working place and an excellent backdrop for attractive accessories such as ceramic storage jars and plants. The granite work surfaces are easy to keep clean, but they are prone to cracking.

There are four basic types of colour scheme from which you can choose:

☐ **Monochromatic:** one colour is used as the basis of the scheme, and variation is provided by different tones of that colour and the use of pattern and texture. However, these schemes often benefit from the introduction of a little contrast colour. A monochromatic scheme is easy to live with and can provide an excellent background for the display of pictures and decorative objects.
☐ **Two-colour schemes:** two related, harmonious colours on the spectrum are used in these schemes – for example, blue and green or green and yellow. The colours do not have to be used in equal amounts, and they can be used in a mixture of strong and light tones.
☐ **Contrasting colours:** two contrasting complementary colours are used to create a strong, dramatic scheme. You may have to vary the tones carefully to achieve an effective balance.
☐ **Multicoloured schemes:** these can be made up of contrasting or harmonious colours or a mixture of the two.

All schemes need some neutral colour to act as a contrast or link. This could be in the paintwork, the ceiling colour or the background colour of a wallpaper or fabric. The use of a few contrasting accents from the opposite side of the wheel can give a scheme drama and vitality.

Bear in mind that bright colours look stronger over a large area and pale colours look paler, and choose a pattern that is in scale with the rest of the room. A small pattern will recede into a blur over a large area, and a swirling pattern will disguise form and contours. Stripes are particularly adaptable. Not only do they have a timeless quality, they mix well with most styles. Pale stripes against a white background look fresh and sunny, while strong, deep stripes look rich and sophisticated. Where natural light levels are low, strong colour intensifies and becomes richer. It is important to remember just how greatly light affects colour, and also that matt colours absorb light while shiny, glossy ones reflect light. Before you finalize any colour scheme, look at samples in daylight and under electric light, during the day and at night.

The conventional starting point for establishing a colour scheme is the flooring, but it could equally well be an interesting fabric, a piece of pottery, a rug, or just a favourite colour or colour combination. The work of great artists can be an excellent source of inspiration – Picasso's 'Blue' or 'Rose' period, the glow of light in Turner's work or the vibrant colours of the Fauvists, for example, could prove a good starting point. Other cultures, too, can provide ideas for a scheme – for instance, the jewel-like colours of India, the soft, faded colours of Tuscany or the warm, earthy colours of American Indians.

CHAPTER SIX

FLOORS AND WALLS

Once you have a colour scheme in mind, you can start to assemble the different elements. Colour, pattern and texture will, of course, be important considerations in your selection, but they, in turn, will be influenced by practical considerations, such as the amount of wear and tear to which these items will be exposed, the budget available and the condition and type of surface to which they will be applied.

FLOORCOVERINGS

After the ceiling probably the largest expanse in the room is the floor, which will have an enormous impact on your scheme. The floorcovering will affect the style, mood and decoration of the whole room and it offers an excellent opportunity to introduce texture. A change in the colour or type of floorcovering is a simple way of dividing up space. You will have to take into consideration the type and condition of the sub-floor to make certain your choice of floorcovering is appropriate and will meet the practical requirements of a particular situation. Give careful thought to the effect that will be created where two floors meet, and how you intend to handle that junction.

There are three main types of floorcovering to choose from – hard, soft and resilient.

HARD FLOORCOVERINGS

These are permanent floorcoverings that are sometimes an integral part of the building. They can be extremely heavy, so you should check that the joists are sufficiently strong to carry the load. If the timbers are particularly springy you should specify that hardboard is laid first. The main kinds of hard floors and their properties are:

☐ **Brick:** is durable and textured but uncomfortable underfoot.
☐ **Ceramic tiles:** are waterproof and hygienic, but they are cold and noisy and will break if something is dropped on them.
☐ **Granite:** is durable, but it is cold and noisy and slippery when wet.
☐ **Hardwood strip:** is attractive, but it is easily damaged and prone to shrinking and cracking.
☐ **Marble:** is beautiful and hard wearing, but it is very expensive, cold, noisy, slippery and heavy.
☐ **Slate:** is durable and waterproof, but it is cold, noisy, slippery and expensive.
☐ **Stone:** is waterproof, attractive, durable and non-slip, but it is expensive and heavy.
☐ **Terrazzo:** is waterproof and durable, but it is noisy, slippery and expensive.
☐ **Tongue-and-groove:** is cheap and attractive and can be finished with paint, stain or varnish.
☐ **Woodblock:** can be laid in a variety of patterns and is inexpensive and attractive.

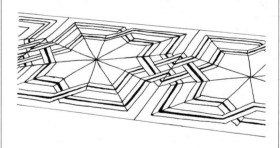

▲ *Terrazzo tiles are expensive but very durable.*

◄ *Ceramic floor tiles can be decorative and practical, but they tend to be cold and noisy underfoot*

► *Wooden floorboards can be the basic part of the structure of a building, but it is also possible to create special effects with woodblock, tiles or parquet.*

►► *Parquet flooring can be laid in a variety of designs, and it can be used as a main floor or as a stunning border.*

SOFT FLOORCOVERINGS

These coverings are soft to walk on, and the main kinds are:

Carpets

☐ Woven carpets such as Wilton and Axminster are expensive but hard wearing, resilient and attractive.
☐ Tufted carpets are less expensive than woven.

57

☐ Carpet tiles can be easily replaced, but they are often not very stylish and can feel rough underfoot.

☐ Synthetic carpets need treating to make them anti-static and stain resistant. Check carefully that they conform to fire regulations before using.

☐ Pile carpets are hard wearing and practical, although those with a longer pile can be easily crushed and difficult to clean.

Wilton carpet is available in a wide range of plains and patterns.

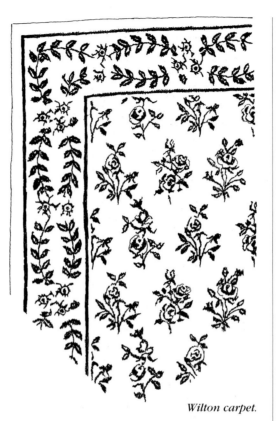

Wilton carpet.

Natural floorcoverings

Natural floorcoverings, such as coir or sisal matting and seagrass, are attractive, fashionable and hard wearing, but they can be rough underfoot, be difficult to clean, harbour fleas and are unsuitable for use on stairs.

RESILIENT FLOORCOVERINGS

These semi-permanent floorcoverings are generally very hard wearing, pleasant underfoot, easy to lay and easy to maintain. It is possible to simulate hard floors, and they can incorporate custom-made designs. They can be supplied in sheet or tile form. Points to consider are:

☐ **Vinyls** can be harmed by grit and cigarette burns.

☐ **Rubber** can be damaged by oils, fat and grease.

☐ **Cork** should be pre-sealed so that it is waterproof and stain resistant. It is prone to fading in sunlight.

◄ *Natural floorings are available in different textures and colourways, and they are a popular alternative to traditional carpet.*

Designs for resilient floorings can be worked out on a computer. A print-out would show the design and list the quantity of tiles and shapes required.

SUB-FLOORS

The condition of the sub-floor will affect the final appearance and durability of any floorcovering you specify. The sub-floor should be smooth, level, clean and free from damp or dust before the covering is laid. Floorboards should be firmly fixed, any gaps between them filled and any protruding nails hammered in. Sometimes the sub-floor will have to be covered with hardboard to ensure that the floorcovering lies well, but it is important to leave access to underfloor pipes and cables. If you intend to use a heavy flooring such as slate or marble, the sub-floor may need reinforcing to carry the weight. This is particularly likely on floors above ground level.

UNDERLAYS

Underlays are used to support the carpet, to prolong its life, to keep in warmth, to insulate sound and to prevent dust penetration from the floorboards. At ground-floor level an extra layer is often used to give further protection from dust. It is essential that an underlay is used with any floorcovering that has a latex backing. Underlays can be of felt or rubber, but whatever the material, they must conform to standards, which include tests for flame retardancy. Foam rubber is used to give a luxurious feel, and some types are specially formulated to make them suitable for use with underfloor heating. On a staircase pads are much safer than a continuous underlay, which could cause accidents.

CHOOSING AN APPROPRIATE FLOORCOVERING

Different rooms have different requirements, and these must be borne in mind before you make your final selection of floorcovering.

Bathrooms

The floorcovering must be non-slip, rot resistant and hygienic. Textured, unglazed tiles are the safest hard floor option. Vinyls work well but linoleum and hardwood can be damaged when soaked. Wool and wool-blend carpets rot and smell awful if moisture seeps into them. In a large bathroom a bordered floor can look stylish.

Living rooms

A comfortable, hard-wearing floorcovering, with a good quality underlay is needed here. The introduction of a border can give definition and variety, while a small-patterned carpet, like a Brussels weave, is a practical choice.

An example of sheet vinyl.

Halls

Always make sure there is an area to catch all the muddy feet coming in. Easy maintenance is an important consideration, and a hard floor could be a practical and aesthetically pleasing approach. If a carpet is chosen, a heavy grade, hard-wearing one would be needed, preferably with some sort of pattern, which would be less likely to show the dirt than a plain colour. The hall floor offers the opportunity to make an exciting decorative statement.

Stairs

The prime consideration here is safety, so carpets must be well laid and patterns that disguise stair edges must be avoided. A carpet that will withstand heavy wear is, of course, essential. If you decide not to use carpet for some reason, avoid slippery or easily caught surfaces, and remember that one advantage of carpet, especially on stairs, is that it absorbs noise.

Kitchens

The floorcovering must be grease and spill resistant, waterproof, durable, non-slip and easy to maintain. Linoleum, vinyl – as long as you avoid light colours – cork and tiles all work particularly well.

Dining rooms

Use an easy-to-clean floorcovering. If you choose a hard floor make sure that it is not too noisy when chairs are pulled in and out and that it is not going to cause anything dropped on it to break.

A patterned linoleum hall floor.

Bedrooms

A warm, comfortable, durable floorcovering is needed, and carpet would be a good choice.

Children's rooms

Choose a practical, tough, warm floorcovering that is easy to clean. Carpet, vinyl and linoleum are all possibilities.

Conservatories

The most suitable floorcoverings are stone, ceramic or terracotta tiles, brick or vinyl because condensation can be a problem. Seagrass matting, which can be cut to fit the room, is a practical choice to combat condensation because it does not trap moisture.

A bordered carpet adds impact to a staircase.

Public areas

The choice is often governed by economy and practicality, although there is frequently the opportunity to incorporate exciting design elements, such as a company logo.

COLOUR AND DESIGN

Scale is just as important on the floor as it is in other parts of a room, and the colour and pattern should be chosen with the size of the room in mind. A large pattern in strong colours will appear bigger and bolder in a small room, while a small pattern in soft colours will fade into insignificance over a large area. Remember, though, that the effect of an intricate or sophisticated design might be wasted if there is a lot of furniture.

You can make an area appear larger by using a plain or self-patterned flooring in cool, pale colours that blend with the furniture and furnishings. Patterned carpets or ones with tweedy, mottled effect are good for disguising dirt. A striped carpet will make a hall appear long or, if the stripes are laid across the floor, wider.

Borders can be used to give definition or to divide up an area visually, and they can also look very smart on stairs. Borders can also be used to make a floor look narrower and add interest to a long corridor.

Many manufacturers now offer a computerized design service that allows them to work with a designer on one-off commissions, such as an original design for a hall floor or the inclusion of a logo into a corporate floorcovering.

Elaborate curtains are not always suitable. Some clients will feel much more comfortable with simple blinds. Dark roller blinds and window frames make a dramatic backdrop to the oriental-style bed and patterned rug.

WALLCOVERINGS

Walls are seen in relation to all the other areas and surfaces of the room, although the line of most walls is broken by doors or windows. There is a wide variety of materials available – wallpaper, paint, fabric, tiles and wood finishes – but before you select a wallcovering there are several points to consider, including the condition of the existing wall surface. It is always worth preparing the surface as carefully as possible. If there is any damp, it must be treated – covering it up and hoping for the best will only lead to further problems – and if you are going to achieve a good finish with paint or wallpaper, the base must be as smooth as possible. It used not to be possible to wallpaper over newly plastered walls, but special types of plaster mean that you no longer have to wait for the walls to dry out.

Paint will allow you to introduce colour and possibly texture into a room, and it is relatively inexpensive, unless you commission a specialist decorative finish, which can add another dimension to a room, giving depth and richness or an extra luminosity. The most generally used paints are undercoat, interior emulsion, which is water based and used for walls and ceilings, and oil-based paint, which is mainly used for woodwork but can also be used for walls and ceilings.

A stencilled floorcloth is an unusual and inexpensive form of floorcovering.

Avoid a gloss finish on walls that are not perfectly smooth.

Wallpaper can introduce pattern, which can be used to create a mood or period style or to give a feeling of intimacy. There is a wide variety to choose from including textured and plain papers as well as those made to simulate wood, fabric, stone, trellis and many other materials. The main types of wallpaper are:

☐ **Lining paper:** gives a smooth base before the main paper is hung or the walls are painted.
☐ **Standard wallpaper:** is available in a huge range of colours and patterns.
☐ **Hand-printed wallpaper:** is very expensive, but it looks wonderful and can give an authentic period feel.
☐ **Vinyl wallpaper:** is intended for areas where there is moisture or condensation.
☐ **Embossed paper:** gives a three-dimensional effect and can disguise or camouflage an uneven surface; it would then need to be painted.

Wallpaper borders give a professional finish and are useful for dividing up large expanses of plain, painted or wallpapered areas and for giving definition.

There are other options for wallcoverings. Walls can be panelled with wood or laminates, covered with fabric or canvas, tiled or mirrored. Wood panels can be pre-cut and fixed to battens or stuck to the wall. The wood used is usually inexpensive and needs painting, which can be done to simulate more expensive wood.

Panelling looks elegant and luxurious, and it can be used to improve the impression of balance and proportion in a room. A panelling effect can also be created with wallpaper. Wood cladding comes in various forms. Simple tongue-and-groove or strips of wood can be nailed together to create panels and fixed to battens, which are then attached to the walls. This method is sometimes also used for the sides of a bath, but usually deal or pine is used, and it must be stained or painted. Wall tiles are a practical choice for kitchens and bathrooms, and they give scope for introducing decorative patterns.

Block-printed wallpaper is expensive to produce but gives an authentic period feel.

▲ *The Chinese Room at Middleton Park in Oxfordshire was decorated in the early nineteenth century in the 'Regency Chinoiserie' style. The key colour in the room is purple, a very fashionable nineteenth-century choice.*
(Christopher Wood Gallery, London/Bridgeman Art Library, London)

▼ *Medieval homes were full of colour – the natural dyes used for fabrics produced rich and intense colours. Fabrics were used to divide up the Great Hall to give more privacy, and were also used to cover chairs, beds and walls, but not windows.*
(British Library, London/Bridgeman Art Library, London)

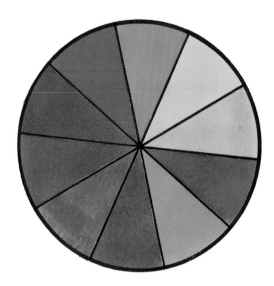

▲ *The colour wheel is the starting point for any colour scheme. Colours opposite one another on the wheel are complementary colours. On one side are the warm, advancing colours and on the other the cool, receding ones.*

◀ *Multi-coloured tribal rugs on the floor, bed and sofa create a warm and harmonious scheme. The pattern of the curtain fabric enhances the rugs and the rough texture of the walls provides additional interest.*
(Fired Earth)

▶ *Red, blue and yellow are the pure primary colours from which all other colours are created. Strong and vibrant, they appeal to children and can form the basis of a stimulating decorative scheme for a nursery or playroom.*
(Anna French Ltd)

◀ *This is an excellent example of a complementary colour scheme. Here red and green give a balanced effect and red accessories provide a visual link. (Interior designer Allison A. Holland ASID; photographer David Livingston)*

▶ *An axonometric projection is an excellent method of showing a whole floor. Here axonometric projections, together with rendered plans, are used to illustrate the layouts for the ground floor retail area and first floor offices of a boutique in Milan. The rendering gives an impression of the surface decoration. (Pamela Pudan)*

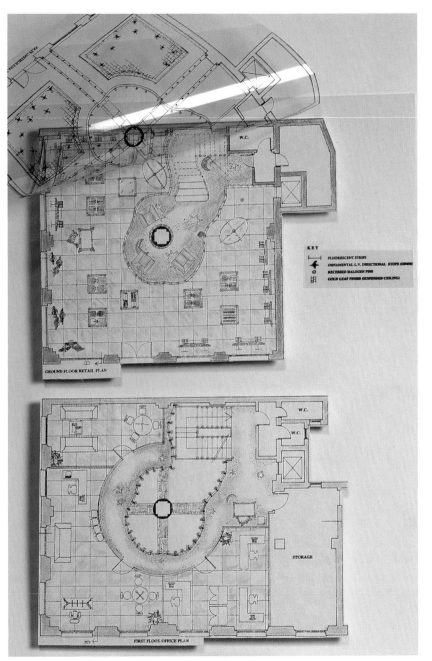

KEY

→ FLUORESCENT STRIPS
◆ ORNAMENTAL L.V. DIRECTIONAL STOPS (50MM)
⊞ RECESSED HALOGEN PINS
▦ GOLD LEAF FINISH (SUSPENDED CEILING)

W.C.

GROUND FLOOR RETAIL PLAN

W.C.
W.C.

STORAGE

FIRST FLOOR OFFICE PLAN

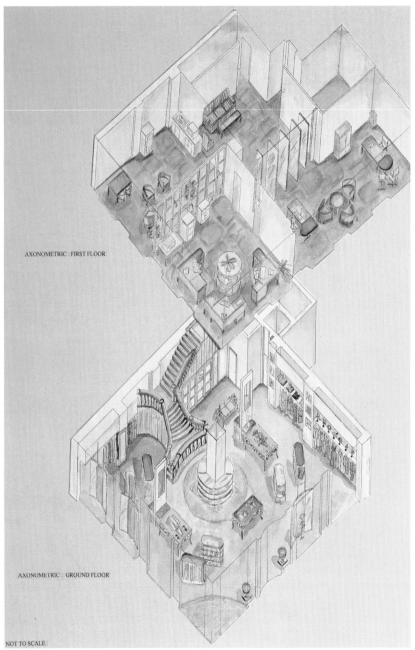

AXONOMETRIC : FIRST FLOOR

AXONOMETRIC : GROUND FLOOR

NOT TO SCALE

PRINTS

CURTAIN FABRIC

BED LINEN

UPHOLSTERY FABRIC

CHAISE LONGUE
FABRIC

ACCENT
COLOUR

◄ ► A client often finds it hard to visualize the finished room. A sample board is a simple but effective device for showing a client how a scheme will look.
(Sue Bramall)

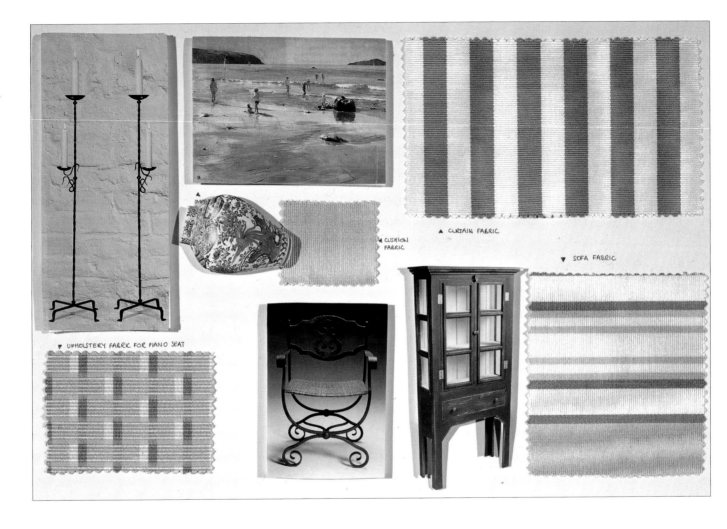

CURTAIN FABRIC

CUSHION FABRIC

SOFA FABRIC

UPHOLSTERY FABRIC FOR PIANO SEAT

◄ *Neutral background colours can be offset by interesting textural contrasts and bold primary coloured accents in this scheme for an apartment. The furniture illustrations are double mounted, which gives a three-dimensional effect.*
(Miriam Hutchinson)

► *A sample board for a café with a futuristic theme. It gives a clear impression of how the space will be decorated and is attractively arranged to appeal to the client.*
(Orla Collins)

Fabric can be used in a number of different ways. It gives a luxurious feeling and adds textural interest. It can be stretched over the wall, fixed to battens, glued to the wall or suspended from a special kind of track. It can also be tented over the ceiling or hung on hooks, Biedermeier style, or used in panels. It is inadvisable to use fabric on dining room walls because the fabric will retain smells.

For other surfaces in a house there is a wide range of materials to choose from, including plastic, tiles, wood, marble or granite.

Placed below a cornice, a wide border can make a high ceiling seem lower, and the addition of another border at dado level, with a practical dark colour below can increase this illusion.

ESTIMATING THE QUANTITY OF WALLPAPER REQUIRED

Measure the height of the room from the skirting board and add the pattern repeat to this measurement to get the 'drop'. Divide the length of a roll by the drop and round the figure down to the nearest whole number. Measure the distance around the room, including doors and windows, and divide that figure by the width of the wallpaper itself. Round up the figure you get to the nearest whole number. Divide this figure by the drop and round up the result to the nearest whole number to give you the number of rolls that will be needed.

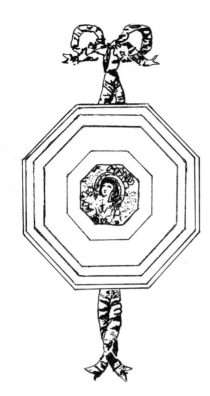

◄ *This charming hand-printed wallpaper is based on an original eighteenth-century design.*

▲ *A variety of paste-on decorations is now available to create garlands, borders and so on.*

65

CHAPTER SEVEN

FABRICS AND SOFT FURNISHINGS

Fabrics are used in a room to give warmth, to absorb noise, to filter light and to soften the architecture, and when it comes to windows there is a huge variety of fabrics, styles and trimmings to choose from.

Windows are an important focal point in many rooms and their treatment is vital to the success of an overall decorative scheme.

The function of the room, the style and mood you want to create, and the budget available will all play a part in influencing your decision, and it is helpful to have a check list to ensure that you recommend an attractive and workable solution.

WINDOWS

☐ Look at the shape of the window, at the amount of wall space and headroom that are available and at the way the window opens and the quality of the view beyond.

☐ Check whether the window is recessed and note the position of the cornice.
☐ Look for any sockets or pipes that might disrupt the treatment.
☐ Note the architectural style of the room and whether there are any particular features that might need balancing, such as a heavy, ornate fireplace.

CURTAINS

Curtains can be single or paired, designed to draw across the window or just to dress it. Dress curtains are a good solution to avoid

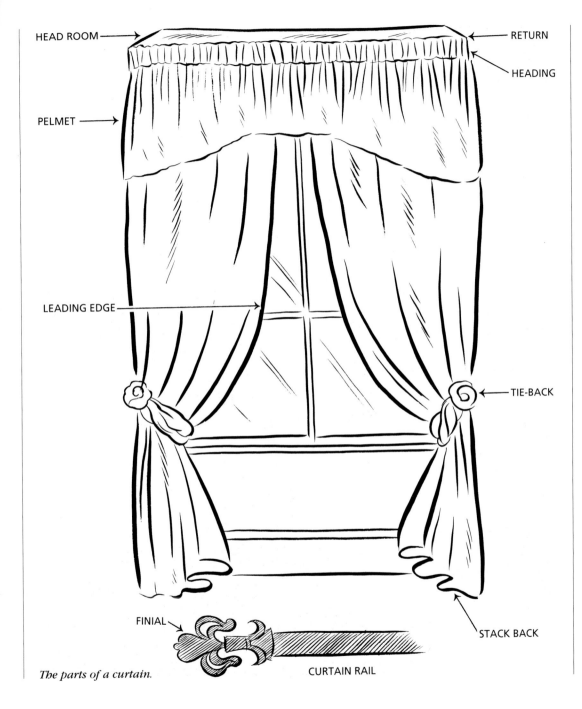

HEAD ROOM

RETURN

HEADING

PELMET

LEADING EDGE

TIE-BACK

FINIAL

STACK BACK

CURTAIN RAIL

The parts of a curtain.

heat loss where there is a radiator. Blackout can be provided with a working blind. Where a curtain heading is going to be hidden or the curtains are not intended for one of the main rooms of the house, pre-made taped headings, in the form of a standard 2cm (1in) gathering tape or deeper pencil pleats, work very well. However, when more complicated styles are required handsewn headings are an advantage because they make it possible to handle greater bulk. French pleats, which are also called triple- or pinch-pleats and in which the pleats are gathered into sets of three, look good in a traditional setting. Box-pleats, which are wide and flat, can be used for valances and loose covers as well as for curtain headings. Smocked headings, which need four rows of stitches, give a charming, countrified effect. Goblet pleats are similar to French pleats, but the top of each one is formed into a short cup or goblet.

PELMETS AND VALANCES

All curtain headings can be used to make attractive pelmets and valances. Stiffened pelmets, for which the fabric is reinforced with buckram, look crisp and smart, and they can be shaped to harmonize with the style or period of the room. Drapery, such as swags and tails, gives a soft, elegant effect. Drapery can be symmetrical or asymmetrical, hung straight or caught back, wound around the pole or draped so that the pole is revealed. The pole itself is often an

67

important decorative element of the window treatment, and it can be made of wood, brass or other metals, while the finials can be in a variety of shapes and styles.

LINING

The lining helps to protect the main curtain fabric, provides extra weight and body and encloses all the hems and raw edges. Although they are traditionally light coloured, coloured linings can be used if they will not show through the curtain fabric. They can look striking, when they are a contrasting or coordinating colour if they are brought round to the front as a trimming. Blackout lining is useful in bedrooms, and a thermal lining, which also blocks out light to some degree, is a useful insulator. Interlining also helps to retain heat in a room and to exclude drafts. It is a soft, blanket-like layer, which is inserted between the main fabric and the lining to bulk out the curtains and improve the hang.

Weights are essential to make curtains hang evenly. These lead discs are inserted into the hem, and concealed in the turnings inside their own individual pockets of fabric.

Cording sets save wear and tear by allowing the curtains to be opened and closed without touching the fabric. An overlap arm takes the edge of one curtain right over the other, giving a sleek look when the curtains are closed.

A stiffened, shaped pelmet.

If two windows are so close together that there is insufficient room for a pair of curtains to each window, you could put a pole across both windows with one curtain at each end. You can use a pelmet or valance with this style if you wish.

A window in a corner may have only limited wall space at one side. Use a blind or a single curtain, caught back on one side.

▼ *When a window and a glazed door are side by side, put a pole or track above both and place a full-length curtain at each end, with a third curtain between the door and the window. Alternatively, use curtains that do not draw at the ends, and fix blinds to the glazing of the door and window.*

▲ *French windows are fairly easy to deal with unless they open inwards. When this happens and where the space and headroom allow, extend the pole or track well beyond the ends of the frame so that the doors can open unimpeded.*

A dormer window projects from a sloping roof; it has a vertical front and sides.

Simple curtains on a track can be used in the recess of a dormer window.

▶ *To stop light coming in at the sides, the paired curtains over this dormer window are held back against the wall by a second pole.*

HOLD-BACKS AND TIE-BACKS

Hold-backs, in the form of brass or wood discs or arms, can be used to keep curtains clear of the window. Alternatively, tie-backs can be made in plaited cord or rope with tasselled ends or in stiffened fabric, usually in a crescent shape. As a rule, the base of the tie-back should be almost two-thirds of the way down the window, though the hook to which it is attached will be higher. Where there is a fixed heading, the tie-backs are often positioned higher to maximize the light, although in some period style treatments they are much lower.

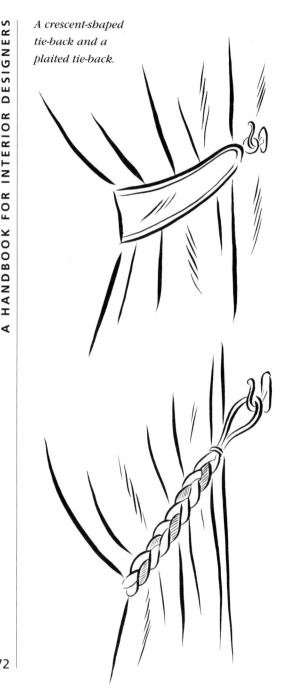

A crescent-shaped tie-back and a plaited tie-back.

BRAIDS

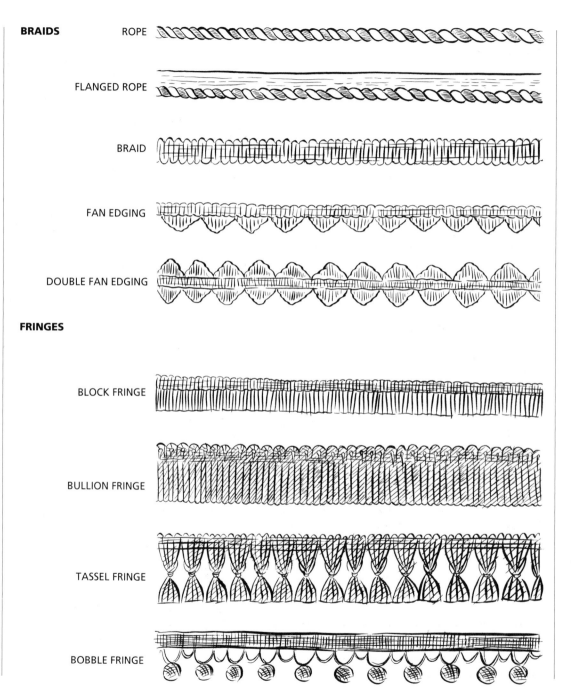

ROPE

FLANGED ROPE

BRAID

FAN EDGING

DOUBLE FAN EDGING

FRINGES

BLOCK FRINGE

BULLION FRINGE

TASSEL FRINGE

BOBBLE FRINGE

BORDERS AND TRIMMINGS

These finishing touches can transform a plain fabric or treatment and give definition and interest. You can use cord, piping, binding, braid or fan edging for this purpose. A plain border can tone down a strong fabric, and even something as simple as ribbon can give a neat, finished edge. A patterned border can lift a plain fabric and, if the weave is not so loose that it catches easily, the reverse side of a fabric can be used as a border. Borders can be double, or even triple, for extra impact.

Fringes on a curtain valance or pelmet give extra depth without cutting out too much light. A bullion fringe will combine successfully with swags and tails, and tassels, rosettes and choux provide a charming way of finishing off headings and tie-backs, and disguising joins.

BLINDS

Blinds can be an effective solution to finishing a window in their own right, or they can be used in conjunction with curtains. The humble roller blind is available in a staggering range of colours, and they can even carry hand-painted designs. Roman blinds, which are corded with horizontal rods at the back, forming lateral pleats when

If curtains meet in the middle of the window on the track or pole and are then caught and tied back, this will have the effect of reducing the width of the window.

◀ *Finials are available in a wide variety of interesting and decorative shapes.*

▶ *Internal shutters can be painted on both sides so that curtains can be dispensed with altogether.*

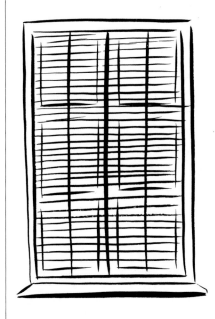

raised, give a smart, tailored look, and Austrian blinds, which are ruched at the base, and festoons, which are ruched down the whole length, give a softer look and are especially appropriate for bedrooms.

Cascade, a softer version of a Roman blind, and London blinds, a less fussy version of an Austrian blind, are both currently popular for interior use.

SHUTTERS

Internal shutters are excellent barriers against noise, cold and, of course, crime, and some older houses may still have their original shutters. Alternatively, shutters can be bought from builders' merchants and specialist suppliers.

If there are working shutters, you might decide to do without curtains altogether, and instead simply to give the shutters an interesting paint treatment on both sides. If you are going to use curtains, make sure that the pole or track extends well beyond the window so that the shutters are free to move.

Fixed shutters look attractive with Roman or roller blinds within the recess of the window. Alternatively, a festoon blind could be hung over the frame.

FABRICS

Once you have decided on a suitable treatment, you can select the fabric. Sometimes, of course, you or the client will find a fabric that you want to use. Then you have to select a suitable treatment for that material. More often, however, you will need to assess the function, style and mood of each room and the amount of wear and tear that the fabric is likely to receive. Different fabrics will suit different locations, and this is an ideal opportunity to introduce different textures, too.

When you choose fabric for curtains, hold it in the way it will be hung. Upholstery fabric does not generally drape very well, although a heavy fabric, with good draping qualities will give a beautifully rich look, and medium to lightweight fabrics will look more

tailored. Remember that fabrics with sheen will reflect light, while matt fabrics absorb light. Pale tones give interesting shadows at night, and dark colours look darker near a window in contrast to the sunlight.

Use patterned fabric with care. In the right setting a pattern can evoke mood and atmosphere, add interest to a scheme and introduce period style. Formal motifs work well in formal rooms, but checks and floral motifs give a more casual feel. Large prints on a big expanse of flat fabric need space around them, but small patterns are lost on a large surface and recede to a blur when seen from a distance.

Patterns can be either woven or printed. Woven fabric, which is excellent for heavy curtains and upholstery, is the more expensive. Screen printing is the most usual

75

and the most cost effective way of printing. Block printing, which is basically a hand process, allows for more individuality and experimentation, but it is, of course, an expensive method.

MEASURING UP

When you need to measure windows to calculate the amount of fabric you will need, add to the length of the track any returns – that is, when the rail bends back towards the wall. Alternatively, measure the pole from finial to finial. You would usually add 8cm (about 3in) for each return plus the same amount for the overlap, if you are using a pair of curtains. The drop measurement will be dictated by the style of heading you plan to use and whether the curtains will hang from a pole or a track. If there is a narrow heading, such as standard tape, the drop would be measured from the top of the rail. If there is to be a deeper heading, such as pinch-pleats, measure from 2.5cm (1in) above the rail. The measurement for a curtain hung on a pole is taken from the base ring.

For short curtains, the track or pole should be fixed as high above the window as the curtains are to hang below the sill to give a balanced look. For long curtains the track or pole should be fixed midway between the ceiling and the top of the window architrave.

To finalize the amount of fabric required, calculate the number of widths required. Most curtains are given a fullness of two-and-a-half to three times the track length, so you would multiply the established track length by two and a half or three, and then divide this by the width of the fabric. It is usual to add 20cm (8in) to the drop measurement for turnings and the hem. Multiply the complete drop measurement by the number of widths required to give the total amount of fabric needed.

BEDS

Bed drapery originally gave privacy and protection from the cold, but these days it has a more decorative purpose, and a draped bed looks cosy and welcoming. There is great scope to design attractive and original treatments for beds. Beds can be dressed simply with a headboard and a valance or bedspread to cover the base. Valances can be gathered or given box-, pinch-, kick- or pencil pleats. Bedspreads can be simple throw-overs or more tailored with box- or kick-pleats.

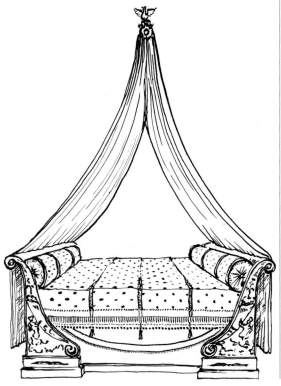

► *A splendid brass bed - complemented by a rich tapestry - is the centrepiece of this bedroom. An unusually framed portrait is suspended in the centre of the tapestry. The chair is covered in a rich damask, the round table with a paisley shawl over lace and the stool at the foot of the bed is covered in a bright contemporary check, showing how successfully old and new fabrics can work together.*

◄ *A lit en bateau with simple draped fabric above. This would work well in an early nineteenth-century property such as the one illustrated on the far left.*

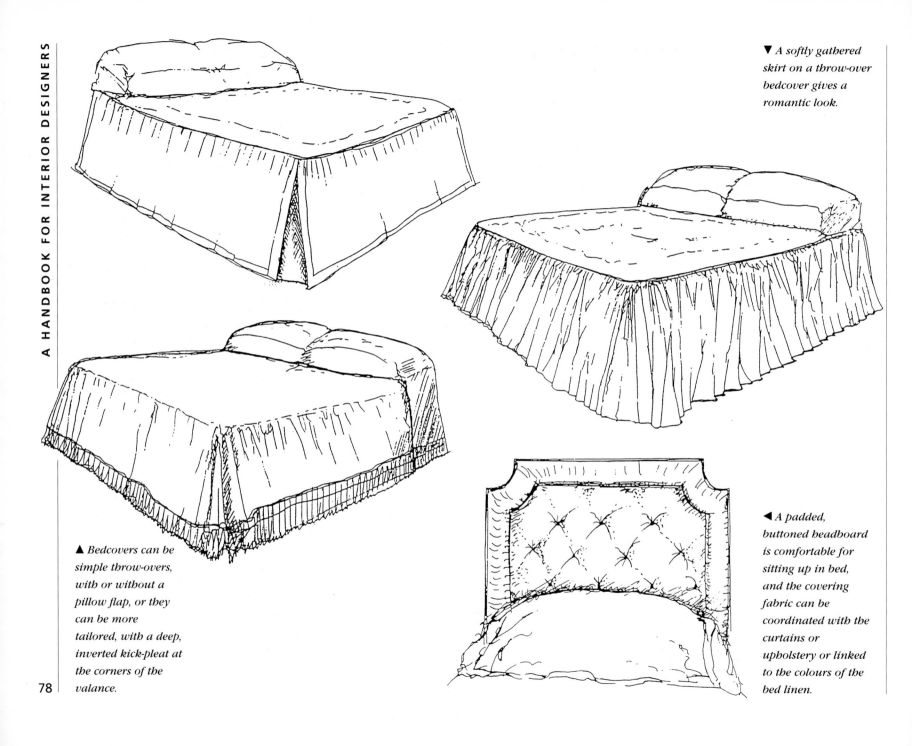

▼ *A softly gathered skirt on a throw-over bedcover gives a romantic look.*

▲ *Bedcovers can be simple throw-overs, with or without a pillow flap, or they can be more tailored, with a deep, inverted kick-pleat at the corners of the valance.*

◄ *A padded, buttoned headboard is comfortable for sitting up in bed, and the covering fabric can be coordinated with the curtains or upholstery or linked to the colours of the bed linen.*

A pillow flap gives a more finished look, and quilting will stop a bedspread looking limp after a year or two.

Bed drapery can range from the simplicity of a single piece of fabric draped over a pole to a fully-dressed four-poster or full-tester bed. Half-tester canopies and coronas, which can be wall- or ceiling-mounted over the bed, are also suitable, especially in period style.

A half-tester can be seen from all angles, so the lining is as important as the main fabric.

UPHOLSTERED FURNITURE

A sitting room usually needs a variety of upholstered items, including one or two sofas, often with a matching chair, one or two comfortable, deep-sprung armchairs, one or two higher, firmer chairs, which can easily be moved around, and an upholstered stool or ottoman. The latter can double as a coffee table if required. All items must conform to fire regulations, and some fabrics will require a special interliner to meet these regulations. You should choose fabrics that are specially recommended for upholstery. You can sometimes get away with lighter weight fabrics on furniture that is not used often, especially if the fabric is lined. You will also have to decide whether to leave legs bare and polished or to provide some sort of skirt, whether it is in fabric or with a fringe. You can choose from loose covers, which can be removed for cleaning and which allow seasonal changes to be made, or close covers, which give a neater look and preserve the line of the furniture. Fabric for loose covers should be tough and firmly woven, colourful and unshrinkable. Good quality cotton, linen union and twill are all suitable, but the fabric should not be so thick that it cannot be stitched when several layers are combined. Suitable fabrics for close covers include velvet, brocade, damask, linen, heavy cotton, twill, wool, needlepoint and leather.

FINISHING TOUCHES

The final details in a room are very important, and they should be carefully chosen and displayed. Decorative objects such as books, pictures, wall hangings, drawings, sculpture and china ornaments usually look best when they are arranged in groups linked by colour, texture or subject matter. Only larger, more dramatic pieces work well on their own. Avoid covering so much of the room's surfaces that the day-to-day function of the room is hampered.

When pictures are displayed consider the picture frame, which is a decorative element in its own right. As with smaller decorative objects, many pictures work well when they are hung together in a group, perhaps linked by colour, subject matter or artist. Before hanging, lay out a group of pictures on the floor to get the desired effect and take into consideration the scale of the room before the final positioning. In a high-ceilinged room, for example, pictures might work well hung one above the other. On rare occasions, a scheme is planned around artwork, but more usually pictures are an accessory chosen to compliment the scheme. Reframing may sometimes be required.

Other details that should be carefully selected to suit the style of the room include door knobs and window catches, light switches and socket plates, bathroom fittings and even waste paper baskets.

With public buildings, a designer will often be required to seek out appropriate accessories. These will need to be chosen with care, not only for their aesthetic appeal, but also for the effect they might have on people using the space. For example, something calming may be used in a waiting area, and something in strong colours for an area where a rapid turnover is required, such as a fast food restaurant. As with all design work, safety is an important factor and decorative accessories must not be placed in such a way as to endanger anyone using the space.

◀ *Striped, unlined fabric for the curtains and bold checks on the sofa give lightness and brightness to this attractive rustic room. The wrought iron pendant light and simple furniture give a cohesive look to the room.*

▲ *Textiles can play an important part in creating the style and ambience of public spaces. Rich fabrics dominate the scheme for a restaurant on this sample board.*

CHAPTER EIGHT

SAMPLE BOARDS

A sample board is, primarily, a visual aid in the communication and sale of your design ideas to your client. It does, however, have a second and serious function. Once the scheme has been agreed with the client, the sample board can be seen as a form of contract, and if a colour or article does not match that shown on the board, you could find yourself in breach of contract. For this reason, if for no other, the titling, or key, is of the utmost importance.

Your board should, therefore, not only be visually exciting but also clear, easy to read and accurate. Above all it should look professional.

PUTTING TOGETHER A SAMPLE BOARD

You will need the following items to put a sample board together:

☐ Featherlite board, kappa board, 3.5mm polyboard for mounting items to give a three-dimensional effect, mounting board
☐ Double-sided tape
☐ Clear, all-purpose adhesive
☐ Rubber-based adhesive
☐ Scissors
☐ Pinking shears
☐ Craft knife or scalpel
☐ Safety ruler, long rule
☐ Mount cutter
☐ Masking tape
☐ Soft pencil
☐ Felt-tip pens, coloured pencils and pens
☐ Dry-transfer lettering
☐ Cutting mat
☐ Velcro for heavy items
☐ White adhesive labels for numbers

THE LAYOUT

All the major items in a room should be represented on the sample board. If the client wants to retain some existing items, a colour match with a paint swatch mounted on the board will enable you to represent the entire scheme. For example, each sample board could have a sample for: ceiling colour, wallcovering, window treatment, upholstery, floorcovering, cushions, bedcovers, lighting and accessories, joinery/woodwork, furniture, ironmongery, design detail, pictures and frames.

There should be a border or frame, equidistant from the edges of the board. The frame itself does not have to be mounted and could simply be an equidistant space all round the edge of the board. You could use a border, ruled in pencil first, and then inked in with felt-tip pen in a colour sympathetic to the scheme you show. Alternatively, dry-transfer tape can be used. A larger space should be left at the bottom of the board for the client's name, which should go on the left-hand side, the name of room or project title, in the middle, and your name and date on the right-hand side. The number of the project to which the board relates should always be shown on the back of the board.

The size and proportion of the samples must be in proportion to their use in the room. For example, the floor and wallcoverings will be fairly large, while cushions and accessories will be very small. There are, of course, exceptions to this rule – items such as paper borders will inevitably be out of proportion on the board if you show them in colour. Although it is possible to reduce them on a photocopier, you could then show them only in black and white.

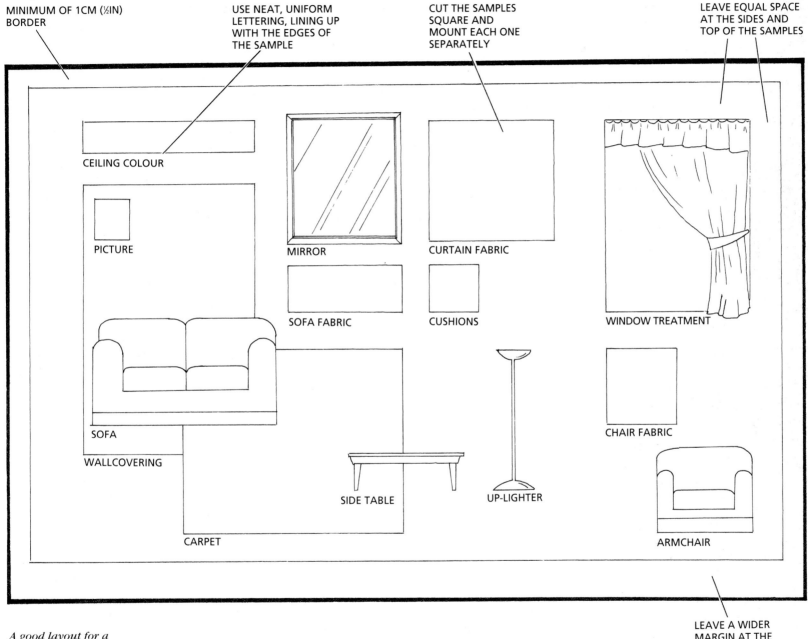

MINIMUM OF 1CM (½IN) BORDER

USE NEAT, UNIFORM LETTERING, LINING UP WITH THE EDGES OF THE SAMPLE

CUT THE SAMPLES SQUARE AND MOUNT EACH ONE SEPARATELY

LEAVE EQUAL SPACE AT THE SIDES AND TOP OF THE SAMPLES

CEILING COLOUR

PICTURE

MIRROR

CURTAIN FABRIC

SOFA FABRIC

CUSHIONS

WINDOW TREATMENT

SOFA

WALLCOVERING

CARPET

SIDE TABLE

UP-LIGHTER

CHAIR FABRIC

ARMCHAIR

LEAVE A WIDER MARGIN AT THE BOTTOM

A good layout for a sample board.

TITLING

You can use either captions or a key to identify the elements on the board.

Captions

It is possible to add captions by lettering directly onto the board. The labels are normally placed under each sample. There should be a uniform space under each item, and the lettering should be aligned with the edge of the sample. Alternatively, you can write or type on adhesive labels and then stick these directly on the board or onto an acetate overlay, which can be attached to the back of the board with double-sided tape.

A key

If you use a key, you should place it at the right-hand side of the board, cross-referencing the numbers on the key with those against the samples. The numbering should begin with 1 at the bottom of the board, with the flooring, and then go clockwise around each board.

Whichever system you choose, the lettering can be done by hand, using pencil guidelines that should be rubbed off when the letters have been inked in, typed onto transparent sheets or done with dry-transfer lettering. If the sample board is for a commercial project, you should make certain that all the samples chosen comply with national safety standards and that this is stated. If you use a substitute sample, state that this is for 'shape' or 'colour' reference only.

MOUNTING THE SAMPLES

The position of each sample on the board is important, and each one should be seen as it relates to the other items in the room. For example, the floorcovering should be at the bottom of the board, as it would be in the room, with the wall treatment and furniture close to it, while the ceiling colour should be at the top of the board. This allows the effect of the colours and patterns to be seen together. It is often possible to see mistakes at this stage, before the schemes are sent to the client.

Assemble everything you are going to use before you start cutting. Pencil in the border, not less than 1cm (½in) from the edge of the board and, if you are using a key, pencil in the shape for this in the centre of the right-hand side of the board and label it 'key'. Pencil lines at the bottom of the board for the client's name (on the left), the name of the room or project (in the centre) and your own name and the date (on the right).

At this stage you should not cut or stick down the samples. Just fold them and work out where you want to position them on the board to create a pleasing, well-balanced effect. Start with the floorcovering at the bottom, place joinery colour, for skirtings, doors and so on above this, and the wallcovering or coverings above this. The ceiling colour should be close to, or above, the wallcovering. Furniture and accessories should be placed next to whatever they relate to – lighting for the ceiling, for

example, should be alongside the ceiling colour while wall lighting should be near the wallcovering. To give a more three-dimensional effect to the board, photographs or drawings can be carefully double-mounted on polyboard.

When you are certain that everything is positioned correctly, remove each sample individually and mark in its position lightly with pencil. Carefully cut each sample to size and shape, and stick double-sided tape on the reverse. If you are using captions, remember to leave enough space to write. Remove the backing tape and stick the sample down. Pencil in the text, and ink it in when you are sure there are no errors. Finally add the border or mount.

PREPARING SAMPLES FOR MOUNTING

Fabric

Stick double-sided tape directly on the back before cutting it to shape. Use pinking shears if the material is likely to fray. Alternatively, cover pieces of polyboard, cut to the right shape and size, with fabric, using mitred corners and keeping down the edges with double-sided tape. This is a good way of showing headboards or upholstery. Fabric for a curtain can be dressed, gathered or pleated to suggest the finished treatment at the top and left to hang loose, with any relevant trimmings or curtain poles to represent the curtain design. Material intended for Roman blinds could be folded.

Carpet

This can be cut with a craft knife and stuck to the board by covering the back with masking tape and then using a suitable adhesive. Rubber adhesive around the edge will stop fraying.

Tiles and wood

Heavy samples can be kept in place on velcro pads. It is advisable to remove these heavy items when the sample board is being transported.

SUBSTITUTES

It is not always possible to find the exact item you need for a board and you may have to use your initiative to solve the problem. Sanitary ware, for example, could be shown by lozenges of ceramic, a mirror by a small mirror from a handbag or powder compact, and stainless steel by cooking foil. The shape of a lampshade could be cut out in the appropriate fabric, and accessories could be cut out from magazines and brochures.

Fabrics have a vital role in decorative schemes and a designer will give careful consideration to the use of colour and interplay of pattern and texture when putting a scheme together.

CHAPTER NINE

PRESENTATION TECHNIQUES

The presentation you make to your client should communicate your design ideas clearly and precisely, give the client confidence by its professionalism and, most importantly, sell the scheme to the client.

Exactly what you show to the client will depend on the size and nature of the project and on what you need to put your ideas across visually. If you have just been asked for a decorative scheme, a sample board will be sufficient, although you might also show the client larger pieces of some of the fabric as well. If a room layout is to be included, a floor plan showing the furniture layout and elevations would probably be required. For more substantial projects you might need to include visuals such as perspectives or axonometrics, rendered to match the samples you propose to use. Nicely presented sketches of small details can be helpful, and it is often appropriate to produce catalogues of furniture and fittings you propose and, of course, to provide costings, which are discussed in Chapter 11.

PLANS

When they are finalized, the plans could be presented on good quality tracing paper (120 gsm) or copied by the dyelined process onto paper. Each plan should have: a title block, which should include your name or company title, address and telephone number, your client's name and address; the drawing title; a drawing number; the scale; the date; and a statement of copyright and a disclaimer. The title block should go at the bottom right-hand side of the sheet and, if you needed to put specification notes on the drawing, this block would be extended into an information panel, running up the right-hand side of the sheet. The title block should be between one-sixth and one-quarter of the overall height of that panel. It is generally best to keep the title panel simple so that it does not detract from the plan itself, but there is no reason why you should not design your own personalized title block. The lettering or type face you use will largely dictate the style.

Most designers have title blocks and panels pre-printed onto sheets of tracing paper. Another method is to have the title block printed on adhesive sheets, which can then be applied to the drawing and the relevant information filled in. These sheets are printed in reverse and should be stuck to the back of your sheet and the information filled in from the front. Alternatively, ready printed architect's sheets are easily obtainable.

If the plan is to be rendered, it can be photocopied or back-traced over the reverse of the plan with a soft, 2B pencil. Turn the plan to the right side on the watercolour paper and hold it in place with masking tape. Re-trace the drawing onto the paper. Use thick watercolour paper, so that you do not have to stretch the paper if you intend to use a watercolour wash.

PEN AND INK TECHNIQUES

One way of adding depth and interest to your plan is by shading. This can be built up with varying degrees of intensity, with dashes executed with a fine nib or heavier dashes, to emphasize the texture and to give a softer effect. You could also use a pointilliste technique to build up the dark

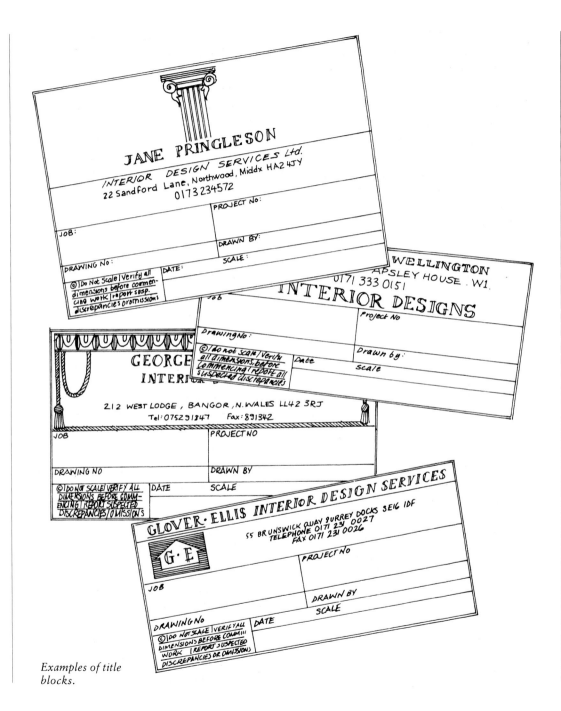

Examples of title blocks.

areas. Soft shadows can be added with pencil by shading on the reverse side of the drawing with a soft pencil smudge. This is particularly effective when the finished plan is dyelined, although it will work after a fashion when it is photocopied.

COLOUR MEDIA AND TECHNIQUES

These techniques are most often used to enhance three-dimensional visuals, but they can also be used to add interest, definition and charm to plans, elevations and sections.

Coloured pencils

An effective way of highlighting drawings and detail work, coloured pencils are quick and clean to use and are available in a wide range of colours. If you do not have time to colour an entire drawing, a 'spotlight' technique can be used, whereby colour is added only to the areas which the spotlight touches.

Watercolour crayons

These can be used in the same way as coloured pencils, or they can be washed over with a wet brush to produce a watercolour effect.

Marker pens

Available in a variety of colours and sizes, marker pens are quick to work with and produce a vibrant result, but they need a delicacy of touch if the design is not to be overwhelmed.

Pastels

Once you are used to working with pastels you will find them quick and versatile to use, and they can be mixed with other mediums. The colour and texture of the paper you use will affect the final result, and pastels must always be fixed with a spray fixative.

Watercolour

This attractive, flexible medium has a pleasing luminosity. Watercolours are available in tubes, liquid form or small tablets, and the liquid variety is particularly vivid. There are two grades of colours, Students and Artists. The Students range is less expensive but, because it is made from lower quality pigments, the colours are less intense than those in the Artists range.

Unless you use very thick watercolour paper, it will buckle when you apply the colour, causing the wet paint to run. The alternative is to stretch the paper, but this is quite time consuming. Mix the colour you want to use on a palette and test it on a piece of rough paper, which must be of similar quality to the one you are using. Coat the areas you are going to wash from the top downwards, tilting the board so that the paint runs towards you. Keep two pots of water to hand, one to rinse your brush and one to thin the paints. If the wash overruns the area you are working on, blot it with clean paper tissues. If the resulting wash is patchy, you have applied the paint too slowly or with too small a brush.

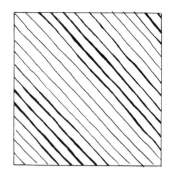

(a) Diagonal lines of different widths give a striped effect.

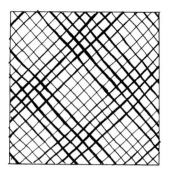

(b) Repeat the technique in the opposite direction to produce a fabric-like effect.

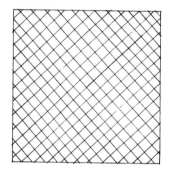

(f) Repeat the even lines to give a solid tone.

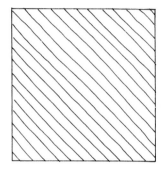

(g) Freehand lines give a more natural, less precise effect.

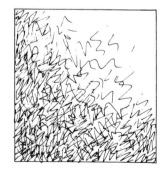

(k) The scribble effect can be used to good effect, especially when it is varied in intensity.

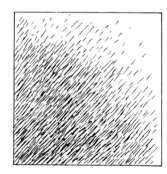

(l) Building up shadows with dashes, drawn with a fine nib, creates texture and shade.

▶ *Pen and ink techniques*

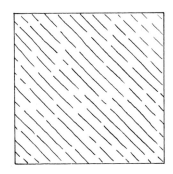

(c) Light, free-hand lines give a softer effect.

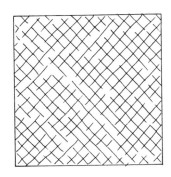

(d) Repeat the light lines in the opposite direction to produce a net-like effect.

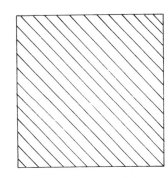

(e) Use a ruler to draw fine, neat lines.

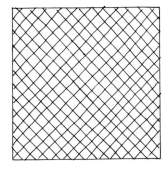

(b) Cross-hatching produces a less formal effect.

(i) This effect was created by using a ruler and three different nib sizes.

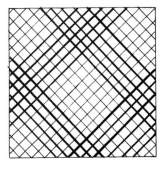

(j) Repeating this technique gives an almost tartan effect.

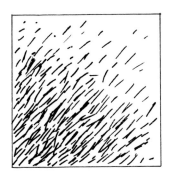

(m) Heavy dashes can be used to emphasize texture and to give a more broken effect.

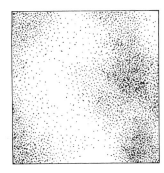

(n) One nib size was used in a pointillist technique to build up dark areas.

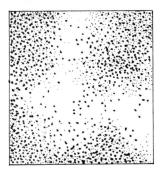

(o) The same technique can be used with various nib sizes to give an effect more quickly.

LETTERING

Poor quality lettering can spoil a whole presentation. Well-executed hand lettering, on the other hand, is attractive to look at and, when you get used to it, relatively speedy to do. It is particularly appropriate for domestic projects, but commercial projects would benefit from a more professional approach, which could be achieved with stencils, transfers or typed lettering.

Hand-lettering

Each letter must be well formed, evenly spaced and unjoined. The size and arrangement of the lettering should be considered in relation to the importance of the legend or caption. Titling, for example, should be large for added emphasis, while subtitles should be small and descriptive notes smaller still. Avoid over-ornate lettering, which will detract from the drawing itself, and aim for clarity and legibility. The primary function of lettering is to provide information. To keep your letters evenly sized and spaced, use a graphed underlay or rule faint, horizontal pencil guidelines, remembering to erase these before the work is presented. The space between words should be just over one letter's width, and at least half the letter height should be left between each line, with slightly more space for lower case lettering so that stems and tails do not cross over. A 0.25 technical pen is a good size for lettering. Most lettering runs from left to right on the sheet and parallel to the bottom edge of the drawing.

Stencils

It is possible to obtain a wide range of letter sizes, type faces and type styles. Clear stencils are the easiest to use because you can see the letters you have already formed, which makes it simpler to plan the spacing. Some stencils are designed so that they are raised above the drawing surface, which helps to avoid smudging the ink.

Dry-transfer lettering

Although the sheets are expensive, dry-transfer lettering gives a very professional finish. It is available in colours as well as in black and white, and there is a wide variety of type faces and sizes.

To transfer a letter place a sheet on the page and rub over the letter with a spatula, brush handle or blunt pencil until it is safely transferred. Handle the sheets carefully, because they are easily damaged, and lift up the sheet gently so that you do not spoil the letters. As with hand-lettering, it is helpful to work within pencil guidelines. If you make a mistake on tracing paper a misplaced letter can be lifted off with drafting tape, but if you make a mistake on paper you will need a soft eraser or even a razor blade or scalpel.

Typed lettering

On small drawings lettering can be typed directly onto the sheet. For larger drawings, the typed lettering can be transferred to adhesive film by photocopying onto the film.

UPPER CASE

ABCDEFGHIJKLMNOPQRS
TUVWXYZ 1234567891O

LOWER CASE

abcdefghijklmnopqrstuvwxyz

Example of hand-lettering.

THREE-DIMENSIONAL DRAWINGS

Many clients find it difficult to visualize how a completed scheme will look from a plan. Three-dimensional drawings will show them how it will look, and when they are rendered, they are particularly appealing and will help to sell the scheme.

AXONOMETRIC DRAWINGS

Axonometric drawings are used to give an interior view from an elevated position and to show what the interior contains. They are particularly useful for kitchens, bathrooms or a floor of offices, which would be difficult to show satisfactorily by perspective.

To draw an axonometric, rotate the plan so that the view you want to draw is at the top of the page. The front two walls are usually omitted from the drawing to allow you to see in. Fix a tracing overlay to the plan and, using a T-square and a 45° set square project the walls at a 45° angle from the plan, rotating the plan by 45° and using vertical lines for the projection. Everything contained within this space must be drawn to scale. When inking in, the exterior walls should be strengthened with a 0.50 nib pen to make the drawing easier to read.

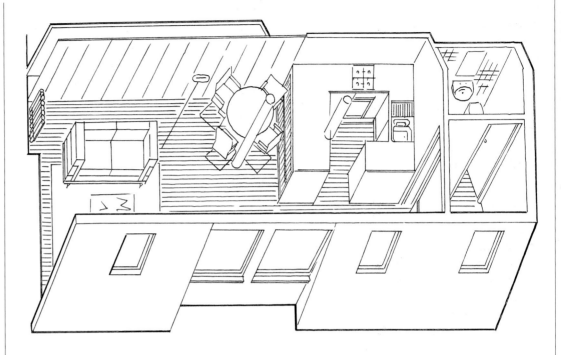

ISOMETRIC DRAWINGS

These work in the same way as axonometrics, but the angle used is 30°. The result is rather more realistic looking, but isometrics are more time consuming to execute because the entire plan has to be redrawn.

PERSPECTIVE

A perspective drawing gives an illusion of depth and gives a client an impression of what the finished scheme will look like. A one-point perspective is the simplest to draw. For this, the room is viewed from a

An axonometric drawing gives an interior view from an elevated position which allows you to show a whole floor. These are useful for awkwardly shaped rooms, which would be difficult to show in perspective.

fixed standpoint, and all lines converge towards an imaginary point on the horizon called the vanishing point. Your eye level acts as a horizon; all lines above this converge downwards towards a vanishing point and lines that are below the eye level will converge upwards towards a vanishing point.

To draw a perspective you will need a pencil, a pen, a drawing board, a T-square and a set square. Decide, first of all, which view of the room you want to show.

1 Fix a sheet of tracing paper over your plan and draw a central line from the standpoint to your picture line, which is the plane on which the vanishing point (VP) is located.

2 Draw an elevation of the back wall to a scale suitable for the perspective and mark in units of 1 metre (3ft) using your scale rule for the height and width of the wall.

3 Draw in the eye level – that is, the horizontal line at which your eye might rest comfortably – and position your vanishing point on that level, placing it further away from whichever wall you want to show most of. To show more of the floor, raise the eye level; to show more of the ceiling, lower it.

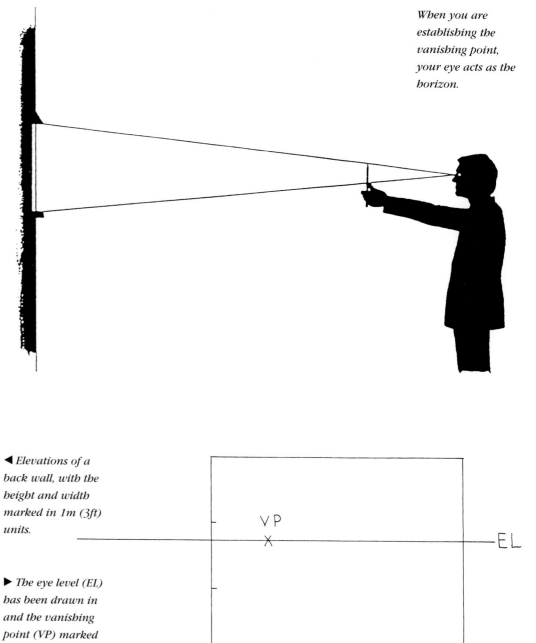

When you are establishing the vanishing point, your eye acts as the horizon.

◀ *Elevations of a back wall, with the height and width marked in 1m (3ft) units.*

▶ *The eye level (EL) has been drawn in and the vanishing point (VP) marked on it.*

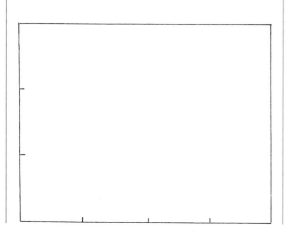

VP
X

EL

4 Line up each corner of the room and the vanishing point with your ruler, and draw from the corner of your elevation outwards, in turn, thereby creating the adjacent walls.

5 Now line up the unit marks (step 2) with the vanishing point and draw lines from these points outwards from the elevation.

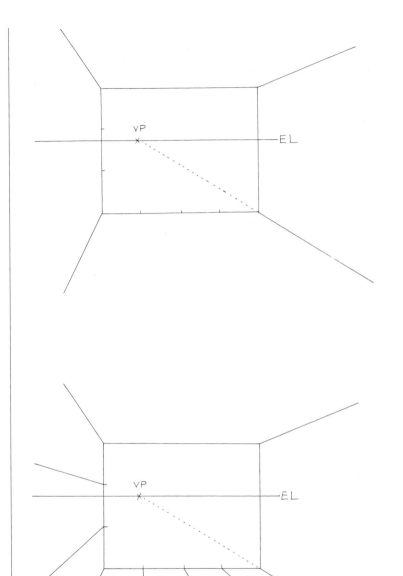

Lines starting at the vanishing point have been drawn through each corner of the room and extended from the corners outward.

Use a ruler to line up the unit marks with the vanishing point and to draw lines from these points outwards from the base and sides of the elevation.

6 From your plan, check the distance you want to show in perspective based on the depth of the room. Using the same scale as the elevation, measure and draw in the depth you want to show, plus one unit, from the elevation side wall furthest from the vanishing point. This end point is called the measuring point (MP).

7 From the measuring point, draw a line through to the nearest lower corner of the elevation and continue drawing it across your floor radiating lines. This is the bisecting line.

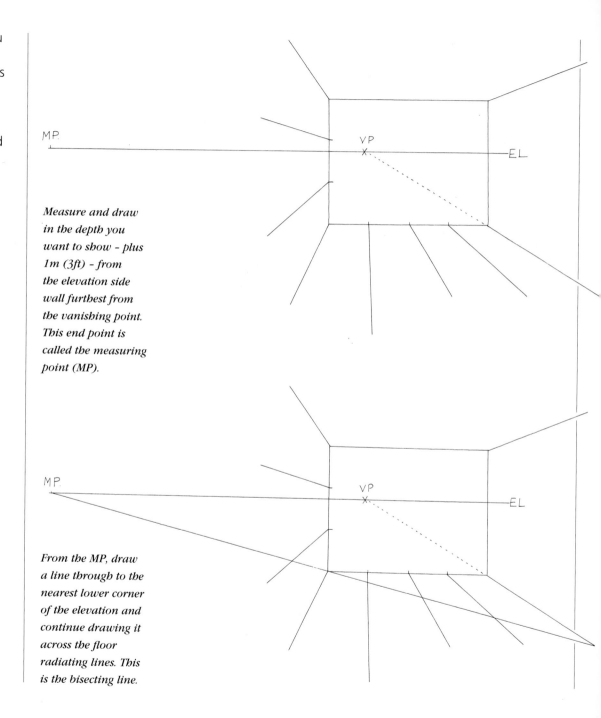

Measure and draw in the depth you want to show - plus 1m (3ft) - from the elevation side wall furthest from the vanishing point. This end point is called the measuring point (MP).

From the MP, draw a line through to the nearest lower corner of the elevation and continue drawing it across the floor radiating lines. This is the bisecting line.

8 With the parallel bar, draw horizontal lines on every junction of this line with the radiating lines to create the floor grid.

9 On the plan, draw a one-unit grid, which will correspond to the perspective you have been working on.

10 Overlay your grid to the plan to cross-refer your furniture layout. Read off the position of items from this grid to work out where they should be drawn on the perspective grid.

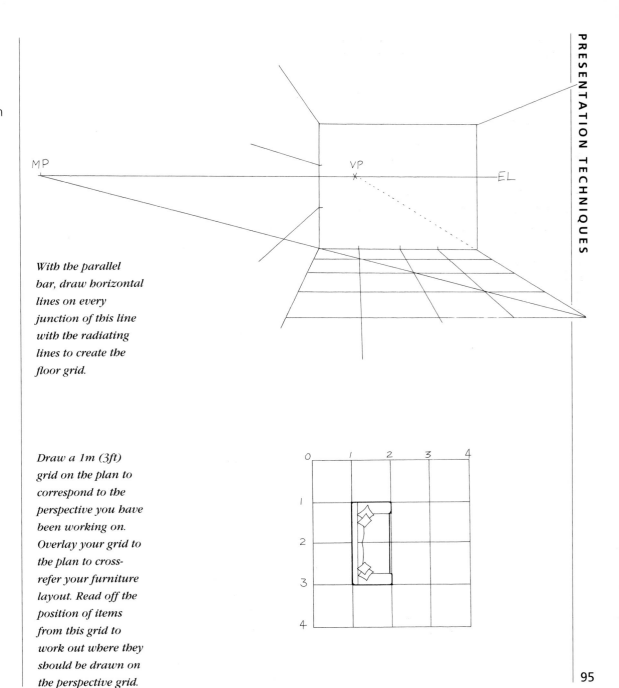

With the parallel bar, draw horizontal lines on every junction of this line with the radiating lines to create the floor grid.

Draw a 1m (3ft) grid on the plan to correspond to the perspective you have been working on. Overlay your grid to the plan to cross-refer your furniture layout. Read off the position of items from this grid to work out where they should be drawn on the perspective grid.

Draw vertical lines from the junction of the side wall and floor to the top of the floor. To complete the wall grids, draw lines from the vanishing point through the unit marks on the side walls.

Draw vertical lines from the corners of the furniture. Calculate the height of the furniture by measuring off to scale the height of the piece on the elevation and then drawing a radiating line down the nearest wall, using the vanishing point.

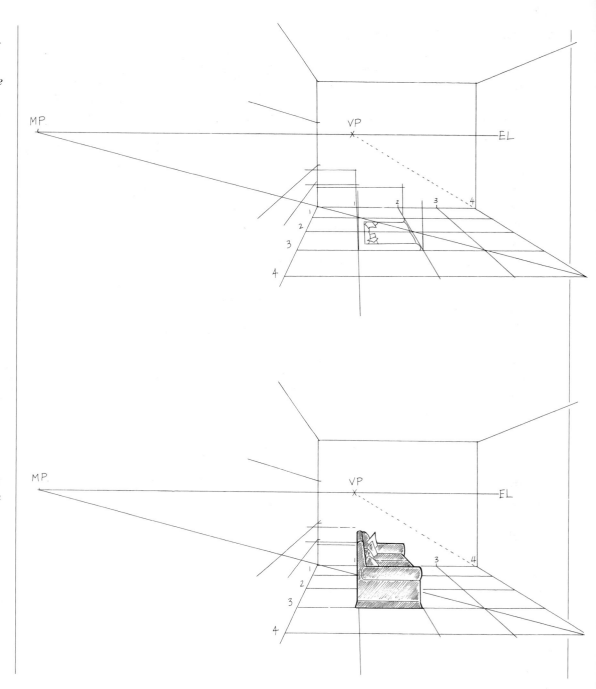

11 At this stage the furniture will appear flat, as on the plan. Use a set square to draw vertical lines from where the side wall meets the floor to the top of the wall. Draw lines from the vanishing point through the unit marks on the side walls of the elevation to complete the wall grids.

12 Draw light vertical lines from the corners of a piece of furniture, which is shown flat at this stage. Measure off to scale on the elevation the height of the piece of furniture and, using the vanishing point as before, draw a radiating line down the nearest side wall. This will allow you to calculate the height of the furniture.

These wall grids are essential, because the side walls cannot be drawn accurately to scale and they allow you to plot in the furniture within the space. It is usual to work in 1 metre or 0.5 metre (3 ft or 1 ft) squares, whichever is the easier to calculate. It is rare that a room is perfectly square, and because you are only giving a visual impression, it is perfectly in order to round the numbers up or down to make your life simpler. The grids should be numbered so that they correspond with each another.

For the final drawing, lay over another sheet of tracing paper and draw in the space and its furniture, omitting the grid lines. This drawing can then be photocopied or back-traced onto watercolour or cartridge paper ready for rendering.

A completed one-point perspective.

97

TWO-POINT PERSPECTIVE

This allows a view of two aspects of an interior – as at a corner.

1 Decide which two walls you want to show and draw a faint horizontal line in pencil as the ground line.

2 Draw a vertical line to show the corner. This should be drawn to scale, taking into consideration that the remaining parts of the room will be larger because they will be in the foreground.

3 Decide where you want the eye level and draw this in. Remember that, as with one-point perspective, the higher the eye level, the more floor will be seen, and the lower the eye level, the more ceiling will be seen.

4 Before positioning the vanishing points, decide which of the two walls you want to see more of and then place its vanishing point a good distance away from the vertical line. The other vanishing point should be placed nearer to the vertical line but should be at least 5 metres (about 5 yards) more than the distance from where you are standing at the edge of the room to the corner vertical line on which the two-point perspective is based. The position of this second vanishing point can be calculated against the unit marks on the ground line. If the vanishing points are placed too close to the vertical corner line, this will distort the floor grid.

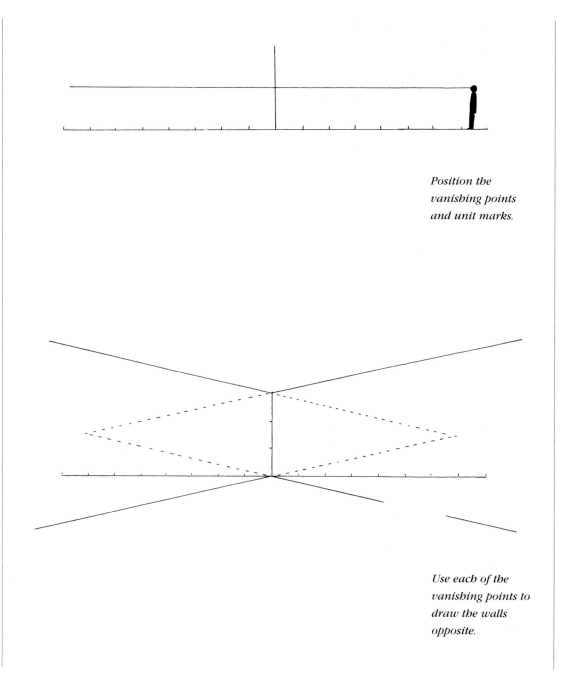

Position the vanishing points and unit marks.

Use each of the vanishing points to draw the walls opposite.

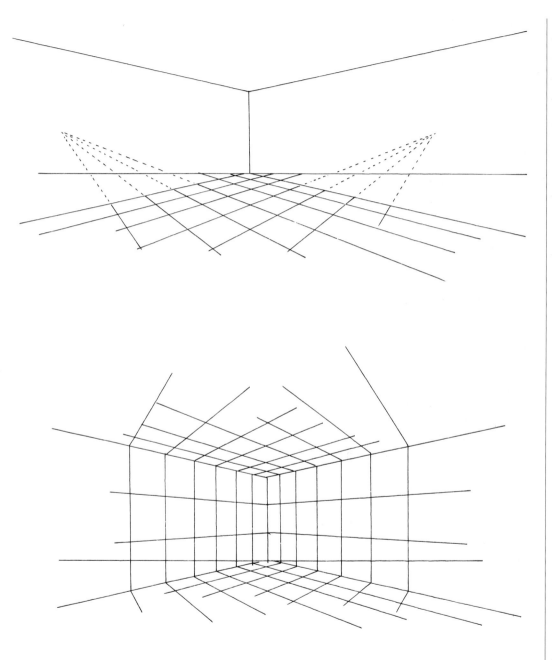

5 Use each of the two vanishing points to draw its opposite wall by lining up the vanishing point with the top and bottom of the corner and then drawing a line, in turn, from the corner away from the vanishing point. This will produce the four walls.

6 To create the necessary floor grid, line up the vanishing points with the unit marks on the ground line, in turn, and then draw from the vanishing point, continuing this procedure across the floor area. Repeat the exercise from the other vanishing point to complete the floor grid.

7 To create the wall grid, draw vertical lines up the walls as an extension of the floor grid. Mark off the corner line in units, and line up the vanishing point with each of these before, in turn, drawing a line through the vertical lines to complete the wall grid.

▶ *Create the floor grid by lining up the vanishing points with the unit marks on the ground line in turn, and then draw from the vanishing point and continue this procedure across the floor area. Repeat from the other vanishing point to complete the grid.*

▶ *(Bottom) The wall grid is created by drawing vertical lines up the walls as on an extension of the floor grid. Mark off the corner line in units. Line up the vanishing point with each of these in turn. Draw a line through the vertical lines completing the floor grid.*

▼ *The ceiling grid is achieved using the same techniques as the floor grid.*

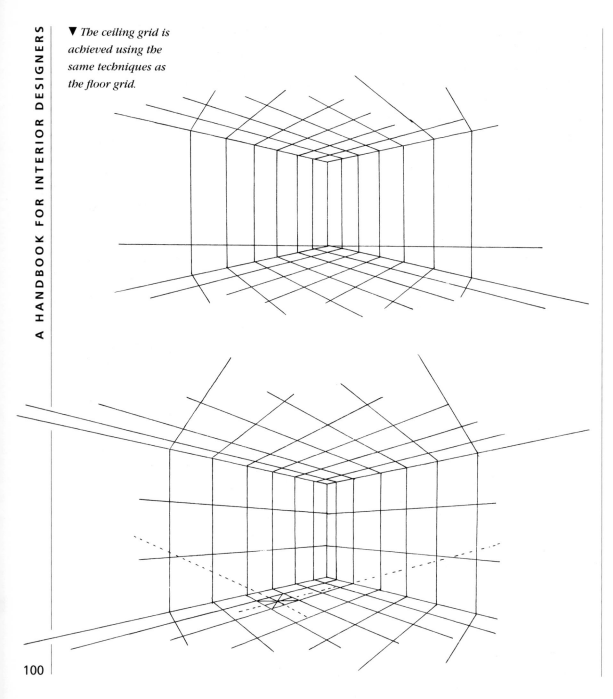

▼ *The position of the furniture is calculated in the same way as for one-point perspective by using a grid over the plan. When you come to work out the height and depth of furniture, you will not have any horizontals to work with. Instead, refer to the vanishing points, remembering that everything happens on the opposite wall. Anything that is shown flat on a wall is governed by the vanishing point on the opposite wall, but if depth is required, you would line objects up with the vanishing point on the wall they would be shown against.*

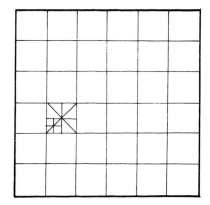

8 Calculate the position of the furniture and other pieces, using a grid over the plan in the same way as for a one-point perspective. When you come to work out the height and depth of the furniture, you will not have any horizontal line to work with. Instead, refer to the vanishing points, remembering that everything happens on the opposite wall – that is, anything that is shown flat on a wall is governed by the vanishing point on the opposite wall. If depth is required, however, you should line objects up with the vanishing point on the wall they would be shown against.

PERSPECTIVES OF PHOTOGRAPHS

A quick way of presenting a proposed scheme is to sketch over a photograph of the existing interior, incorporating any changes you would like to make. The photograph can be enlarged if necessary. The resulting drawing can again be photocopied or back-traced onto paper for inking or rendering ready for presentation.

PHOTO-MONTAGE

Photo-montage is basically a time-saving technique by which trees, figures, furniture and objects can be included in artwork by using photographs cut from newspapers, magazines or catalogues. These can be glued directly onto a drawing, which could then be photocopied, or they can be photo-transferred. This works best with colour photographs stuck onto less glossy paper. Paint the back of the photograph with white spirit or methylated spirits, then place the image to be transferred face down on the artwork and work over it with a soft, blunt pencil to transfer the image. The original can then be peeled off and should leave a soft, subtle image behind.

A less precise, but nevertheless effective form of montage is collage. Torn pieces of paper or other materials are glued to a board to create a variety of effects. This can be a useful presentation tool when it is used to convey the mood or atmosphere of the scheme you are about to present. This type of collage is one that can be used to give a client a feeling for the atmosphere of a scheme you are about to present. These are referred to as concept boards. Collages can also be a form of decoration mounted on the walls.

MOUNTING

Drawings and artwork that are mounted on boards or thick card are easier to handle, have more impact and look more professional. The colour of the board should be chosen so that it complements rather than overwhelms your work. If necessary, drawings can be trimmed to give a neat edge and then carefully glued to the board. Service plans can be mounted on their own board or they can be shown as an overlay to the plan. Velcro pads can be placed at the top edges of the plan and the overlay so that you can simply put the overlay in place when you are ready to talk about it.

WINDOW MOUNTING

Window mounting involves cutting a hole in the mounting board and fixing the drawing to the back of the board so that it is viewed as through a window. Experiment by placing four pieces of card around the artwork until you achieve the desired frame size and all the edges are square. Mark off each corner with a soft pencil, then trim the artwork so that it is about 12mm ($\frac{1}{2}$in) larger all round than the walls. Place the work the right way up on the mounting card. Ideally, a mount has equal margins at the sides and top and a slightly wider border at the base. Use a steel pin to mark the location of the artwork through each corner of the image and then remove the artwork.

Cut the mounting board with a craft knife against a metal straight edge, working on a cutting mat. Line up the metal straight edge on the pin holes and cut out the window. Neaten the corners with a sharp blade and, if necessary, smooth rough edges with fine glasspaper. Stick a piece of double-sided tape across each corner of the back of the artwork and place it, face up, so that the sticky side of the tape is facing you. Then gently lower the mount into position. Turn over the mount and secure the artwork with more tape.

REPRODUCING ARTWORK

PLANS AND ARCHITECTURAL DRAWINGS

The traditional method of reproducing plans is the dyeline method, which can faithfully reproduce pencil, pencil shading tones and fine lines. It is not expensive, but it can give a very dark background. Copying onto plain paper is a quick, flexible method that is suitable for work that is not too dependent on fine detail.

The zoom facility on a photocopier can also be used to enlarge and reduce drawings and graphics and even to rescale plans. Old or damaged drawings can be recopied to produce a clean copy with enhanced detailing, and drawings can be cut and pasted into new compositions for presentation purposes.

COLOUR COPYING

Colour laser copying is relatively inexpensive and gives a good quality result. Bubble jet copying is expensive, but it can produce larger format work than the laser method. Alternatively, work can be colour copied by photography but this is usually best done by a professional, and is, therefore, quite expensive.

When the visual side of a presentation is complete, it is worth spending some time listing the points you want to make and the order in which you want to make them. Decide whether you will show the client the whole scheme at once or bring out pieces of the presentation singly. Make sure you are familiar with the figures and be prepared to make alternative, cost-cutting suggestions. Spending this extra time can make all the difference to the success of the presentation.

Once you have drawn your final plan, decide which method of reproducing the plan will give you the best results.

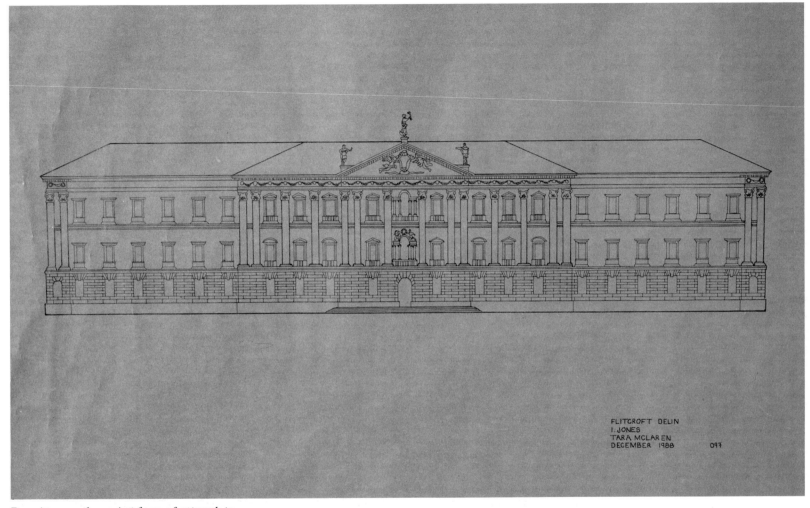

FLITCROFT DELIN
I. JONES
TARA MCLAREN
DECEMBER 1988   097

*Drawings are the easiest form of artwork to
reproduce without losing quality. A drawing
like this can be enlarged or reduced as required.*

CHAPTER TEN

MANAGING THE PROJECT

Once the client has confirmed acceptance of your schemes and agreed your terms of business, you move on from the preliminary stage to project management. You will need to work out a detailed timetable in order to do this efficiently and to ensure a smooth sequence of work.

The first step is to allocate the project a reference number and open the necessary paperwork. Draw up contracts with your workforce and supply them with detailed specifications and with drawings and plans where appropriate. (Examples of specifications are given on pages 107–8.) Agree with your suppliers and contractors how long they need to carry our their particular part of the work and build this into a timetable.

Bring in professionals for construction if it is required, and apply for any permissions that may be necessary. If there is any doubt in your mind about the structural state of the building when you carry out your initial survey, you should insist that a structural surveyor is brought in to report and advise. Similarly, you should never allow a client to persuade you to take on work that should be carried out by an architect. Safety should be a priority: the safety of the site and the workforce, and the safety of the client in the completed project.

Check that the client is properly insured, particularly if scaffolding has been erected, because extra insurance may be required. You should also check that your own insurances are in place.

Arrange skips if they are needed and obtain permission from the local council if the skip has to be placed on a public road. Where it is impossible to place a skip, contact one of the specialist companies that will collect building rubble from an agreed point at an agreed time. Insist that the builder uses chutes if rubbish needs to be brought down to the skip from the top of

the building. Establish where building materials can be stored, what services will be available on site and that access is available within working hours. Check parking arrangements for contractors, and if their parking has to be paid for on a daily basis, allow for this in the project costings. It can mount up to a substantial sum.

Orders can be placed at this stage for flooring, furniture and fabrics, although it is wise to delay ordering any finishes until the bulk of the structural work is complete in case any changes are made. The major structural work might include re-roofing, knocking down walls, taking out or putting in a fireplace, replacing windows, repairing or installing floors, plumbing, rewiring and installing electrics and lighting. Plastering would follow, and then the preparation for decoration. It is usual to start at the top of the house and work down, beginning with the ceilings in each room. Floor sanding and the installation of joinery and built-in furniture should be done between preparation and final decoration. Surface flooring can then be laid, and finally the curtains can be hung. The site is then ready for the delivery of furniture and the addition of any accessories. Remember to notify in advance companies making deliveries if there are several flights of stairs or if access is difficult. It is advisable to check any orders you have placed a week or two before delivery is due to make certain that everything is on target.

While the project is underway, you should visit the site as often as possible and keep your client fully informed of the progress. Be prepared for problems to arise on site. Even with the best laid plans, these are sometimes unavoidable. When a project runs into unforeseen difficulties, the morale of the workforce may be low, and it is essential that you make regular site visits and are seen to take clear, well-thought-out decisions if necessary.

Make sure that you present the interim invoices to the client at the agreed stages and pay the contractors and suppliers promptly. Your relationship with your workforce is very important. If they are unhappy with arrangements and their workmanship is poor, it will reflect on you. Properly and considerately handled, they will give their best.

Project management requires attention down to the last detail. The work at this gentlemen's hairdresser began with the installation of basics such as the plumbing and ventilation and was carried through to the final display of goods.

CHAPTER ELEVEN

PROFESSIONAL PRACTICE

Almost inevitably, a large part of an interior designer's work is administrative. A good interior designer is not only required to produce an exacting response to a brief with creative ideas, but to ensure the smooth running of every project, whatever its size, to organize their workforce so that both client and workforce are happy to complete the job within a specified time scale and to budget, with the minimum of mess and disruption.

To achieve this you need an organized office and methodical paperwork.

FILING

You will need to set up a personalized system whether you are using standard files or disks. Each project will need its own file, with separate sections for some or all of the following: correspondence, schedules, barchart/timetable, specifications, estimates, orders and a master sheet for payments in and out. Each project should be allocated a reference number, which should appear on all related paperwork, drawings and presentation work.

REFERENCE MATERIAL

Once a project has begun you will find that there is little time to do general research, and so you need a good reference library. You could divide this into three main sections:

Professionals

Apart from the obvious categories, such as insurance, bankers, solicitors, customs and excise and accountants, this could also include related professional associations such as those for designers, interior decorators and decorators, and any other professionals whose help and input you might require on a project, such as architects, chartered and quantity surveyors or lighting consultants. You should also keep up-to-date records of local survey and fire officers, and environmental health officers.

Contractors

Keep up-to-date addresses and telephone numbers for builders, plumbers, electricians, gardeners, specialist decorators, curtain makers and upholsterers.

Suppliers

Probably the most efficient way of keeping information on suppliers is in the form of index cards, cross-referenced with the suppliers' catalogues themselves. You will need to have good reference material on lighting, furniture, fabrics, decorative accessories, glass and mirror, flooring, wallcoverings, bathroom and kitchen fittings and partitioning. You may also, of course, have some actual wallpapers and fabric books, which should carry your name and up-to-date prices.

Finally, you should keep inspirational reference material. This might best be organized under room categories, so that if you saw an exciting office layout or a striking bathroom design in a magazine or catalogue you could file these under 'Offices' and 'Bathrooms' for future reference.

RECORD KEEPING

You must keep clear and accurate records of a project from the first explanatory telephone call from the client. Whenever you take a decision or make an alteration, confirm it in writing, because clients, contractors and suppliers do not always remember everything you have told them.

Every project should have a timetable, starting on the day it was contracted, and showing the target completion date, with the movements between all the various contractors involved with the project. An effective way of doing this is on a bar chart, with different colours used for the different rooms, and the times that various activities should take place there clearly shown. You will also need to keep a running record of the progress of the project, which is an invaluable support system and point of reference. This would include full details of the client, the contractors, the suppliers, any professional advisors (including all names, addresses, telephone and fax numbers), and an outline of the brief. It should also include a note of any action taken and the date. Never fall into the trap of relying just on memory.

Schedules

You should also draw up schedules, which can be laid out by room or by subject. These should include details of existing furniture and accessories, the furniture and accessories to be purchased, wallcoverings, floorcoverings, paintwork, joinery, bed and window treatments, building, electrical and plumbing work to be carried out.

You must also keep a record of the decorative scheme for each room, together with the names and reference numbers of fabrics, wallpapers, trimmings and floorcoverings and a small sample of each item stapled next to the details.

Orders

Because the orders record your instructions to suppliers, they must be clear and accurate. A written order is another stage in the smooth progress of a project, and it should include full details of your company, the order number and date it was placed, the project reference number and contract name, the supplier's details and contact name, a description of the goods (name, reference number, size, finish, trim, quantity required, price), the batch/roll/stock numbers, with samples attached if an exact match is required, delivery address, dates and cost. State if this is confirmation of a verbal order, if the goods have been previously reserved and if your approval is required at any stage of the production.

SPECIFICATIONS TO CONTRACTORS

You are totally reliant on the quality of work and service that your contractors give, so it is essential to find the most appropriate and reliable workforce and specialists for a particular project. You should never allow a client to persuade or pressurize you into undertaking an unrealistic timetable because this is unfair to your contractors and puts the quality and professionalism of the whole project at risk.

The workforce can only do their job well if you look after them properly. First, this involves giving them clear written instructions and, where appropriate, plans or drawings. These instructions are usually referred to as specifications and, like schedules, they can be done on a room-by-room or on a subject basis. They should be clear and detailed and always include names and reference numbers of the items involved. Next, you should manage the financial structure of the project so that contractors and suppliers can be paid on time. On larger projects you will need to draw up a proper contract with your workforce which is when they become 'contractors'. There are excellent contracts available for this purpose from designers' professional associations.

Sample specification

A specification is a clear statement of your intent on a room-by-room basis. The following sample specification is to a curtain maker, and you should give a copy to the client, keep a copy in your files and probably give one to your curtain maker, particularly if he or she is working on more than one room in a project. You will find that the two most useful forms of specification are for soft furnishings and decoration, but they can be used for many different aspects, such as joinery, bathroom fittings, ironmongery and so on.

☐ **Floor in house/flat:** Ground, first, etc.
☐ **Room:** Bedroom, dining room, etc.
☐ **Curtain treatment:** give a clear, detailed description of the treatment, including floor length, lining and interlining details; style of heading pelmet or drapery and method of suspension. For example, one pair of full-length, lined and interlined curtains with

French headings. Curtains to be hung from a track concealed by a matching, fabric-covered board which is to be fixed 10cm (4in) above the head of window. Curtains to be dressed back with brass rosettes.

☐ **Curtain fabric reference**
☐ **Width and repeat**
☐ **Supplier** (including address and telephone number)
☐ **Contrast fabric reference**
☐ **Width and repeat**
☐ **Supplier** (including address and telephone number)
☐ **Trimmings reference**
☐ **Supplier** (including address and telephone number)
☐ **Floor finish**

ESTIMATES

Your estimates must be clear, straightforward and above all, accurate. Everything must be checked and rechecked before it is sent to a client, because any error would be unprofessional and would undermine the client's confidence in your ability to do the job.

▶ *An example of a curtain estimate submitted to a client.*

Sample curtain estimate

HALL
To:
Make 1 pair of lined and interlined curtains, with a machine pencil-pleat heading

Make 1 pair crescent-shaped tie-backs self-piped

Make 1 stiffened shaped pelmet

Supply white lining

Supply interlining

Supply 33m/yd 'Garden Ribbon' fabric at X per m/yd

Make 1 pair of voiles to the floor, machine tape heading and hems

Supply 25m/yd of co-ordinating 'Garden Ribbon' voile at X per m/yd

Supply and fit pelmet board with 2 sets of Kirsch corded tracks

Hang and dress curtains, voiles and pelmet

Cost

STUDY
To:
Make 2 Roman blinds to be fitted 30cm (12in) above recess

Supply lining

Fitting (to include brass hooks)

Supply 8m/yd 'Palladian Stripe' at X per m/yd

Sub-total

DINING ROOM (front window)
To:
Make 1 London blind with rosettes to fit onto architrave

Supply lining

Fit London blind

Supply 11m/yd 'Ochre Damask' fabric at X per m/yd

Sub-total

Sub-total

Total

Signed . . . . (For client to sign, date and return with cheque)

Date . . . .

Cheque for 50% herewith as deposit . . . .

THE ACCOUNT

When the work has been carried out – in this case, when the curtains and blinds have been put into position – and the client is happy, a final account is sent. Because the estimate you sent was so detailed, a simple statement, such as shown, is all that is needed.

▼ *Your final account need not be detailed, as shown in the example below.*

```
        Your name or company name, address and telephone number


Name and
address of
client

Date
                           FINAL ACCOUNT

To: Supplying goods as per estimate dated . . . . . . . . . . . . . .




      Less paid on account

        Balance due

Terms: 14 days
```

FEES

While there are no hard and fast rules on charging and no set scale of fees, three main methods are generally accepted. Although you must make certain that you charge fairly at all times, do not fall into the trap of forgetting to take into account any overheads you may be carrying or including the amount of time the work actually takes.

Mark-up

The mark-up derives from the purchase of goods at wholesale or trade prices that are sold to the client at retail prices. On a project for which a lot of goods are supplied, the decorator will make a large part of his or her profit on the mark-up – that is, the mark-up on the costs of goods and services supplied. With highly priced goods, especially when they are supplied in quantity, these mark-ups can be substantial, and they should be taken into account when the overall project costs are estimated.

You make your mark-up by the sliding scale of discount given by the manufacturer. This varies from 10 to 40 per cent, and will depend on the volume and consistency of your account. If you operate this method, you should ask for 50 per cent in advance. An initial design fee may also be charged, possibly deductible from the final price, if the project goes ahead.

Design fees

Design fees are charged either at a one-off sum, agreed with the client, or as a percentage of the total cost of the project.

If you adopt the latter method, the fee can be calculated on a sliding scale, as architects charge, so that the higher the cost of the job, the lower the percentage of the design fee. Percentage payments are made at pre-agreed stages of the project. The first amount is always paid at the outset and the final payment on completion, but the intervening payments, called stage payments, will depend on the size, length and complexity of the job.

On a large project, a client may retain a small percentage for an agreed 'snagging' period, during which the designer will agree to undertake any necessary repairs resulting from the works, such as minor cracks, rucked carpets and dropped curtains.

Hourly rate

This is a variable sum, mutually decided between designer and client, and it is a particularly useful method for consultation work or for buying furniture and decorative accessories. If the arrangement includes travel costs and expenses, remember to keep all receipts.

OPENING ACCOUNTS WITH SUPPLIERS

You will find it advantageous to limit accounts with suppliers to a few large accounts in order to keep the paperwork down. It will also enable you to form good working relations with some important suppliers and to establish your credit rating.

FINDING YOUR CLIENTS

Clients often come from word-of-mouth recommendation from satisfied customers who, in turn, will recommend your services to their friends and colleagues. Advertising is a possible, if expensive, option but an article about you in a newspaper or magazine is a particularly effective way of becoming known because it will be seen as an endorsement of what you do and give a prospective client confidence. You could approach your local newspaper or a home furnishing magazine direct or contact some freelance journalists with a view to their writing about your work.

Another possibility is to contact all your local builders and property developers who may be able to use or recommend your services, and you could also leave your card with local estate agents so they can pass your details on to purchasers who may be looking for an interior designer.

It is important to have business cards with you at all times, because leads often emerge on social occasions or when you are attending exhibitions or doing research. Try to avoid working for friends, but if you do, make no concessions and run the project in a professional and business-like manner.

If you are looking for work as part of a design team for a company, you will need to put together an appropriate portfolio. You should also give a lot of thought to your CV and letter of application – this sort of work is highly competitive and yours will need to be outstandingly well presented if it is to open up any opportunities for you.

Although design work often involves long hours and considerable stress along the way, it enables you to combine your creative and organizational skills in a unique way and the client's pleasure on completion of a successful project is the ultimate reward.

INDEX